Our Lady of the New Millennium

One Man's Dream

Gail Jardine

JMJ Home Corporation, St. Charles, Illinois

ISBN 978-0-9801567-0-6 – Hardcover
ISBN 978-0-9801567-1-3 – Softcover

Photo credits: Special thanks to all those who have contributed photographs or other artwork to this book, especially the following:

Oscar Mendez
Frank Smoczynski
Michael Cheney
Charles Parks
C. McDuayne
Sam Lucero / www.samlucero.com
James Krischokas
The children of St. Hedwig School, Wilmington, Delaware

Published by JMJ Home Corporation, St. Charles, Illinois

Design and layout by MorningStar Media Group, Ltd.

Printed by RR Donnelley
Printed in the United States of America

Acknowledgements

My Special thanks to Frank Smoczynski who knew this was a story that should be told, and who contributed throughout the process to make sure that it happened.

And to Rebecca Nichols who spent many hours doing whatever was needed to make the book a reality.

And very special thanks to a very special lady, Francine Demma. Not only did Carl's story that she shared inspire me; her own story is a true inspiration. And in the process, I had the great good fortune to make a very special friend. Thank you, Francine, for your generosity and everything you have contributed to help Carl build his statue, and share the story with so many others.

Gail Jardine

Contents

Part I

Part II

Foreword

This is the story of a man and his lovely lady. It is a story of beauty and inspiration, of dedication and awe. It is a story of faith and determination, imagination and love. This is the story of Carl Demma and Our Lady of the New Millennium.

Preface

The first time I met Carl Demma was when he came to the Archdiocesan Offices to tell me about a colossal statue of the Blessed Virgin Mary he had commissioned. I had been less than a year Archbishop of Chicago when he wrote to tell me about his project, and I was intrigued. He was a man completely in earnest and completely certain that this statue would be a source of blessing for thousands of people.

During that meeting, his sincerity was palpable, as were his devotion to the Blessed Mother and his confidence in what he believed God was asking of him. His wife, Francine, sustained him as much as did the faith they both shared.

Objections were never obstacles that might stop the work, only challenges to be overcome. In time, all the obstacles were overcome, and the statue was incorporated into the Archdiocese of Chicago's celebration of the New Millennium. Her title comes from that moment of history when Pope John Paul II brought the Church into the third millennium of her existence and made the marking of time into an occasion of renewal of the apostolic faith.

If Carl loved the Blessed Virgin, Mary also loved Carl. The many sufferings of his life seemed only to deepen his union with God and with those whom God had given him to love. Stories of graces received and favors granted make it clear that God accompanies us with His loving providence. The divine love breaks through more forcefully when God's care becomes evident in wonders and even small miracles. Those who love God's only begotten Son have always gone to the Mother of Jesus for help. By baptism, we are Christ's brothers and sisters, and his Mother is also ours. This book is a tale of this love in story after story.

The last time I saw Carl was in Holy Name Cathedral. He had remained in his pew at the back of the cathedral after Mass, and I didn't talk to him then because he was talking to the Lord.

A few days later he was abruptly called to the Lord. Despite the shock and sorrow of his sudden death, especially for Francine, it occurred to many of us that Carl's death meant he would finally be able to realize just how grateful so many people were to him, just how much he was appreciated. Most of all, I can imagine Jesus himself thanking Carl for honoring His Mother.

The story of Our Lady of the New Millennium didn't end with Carl's death. It won't end as long as men and women love the Blessed Virgin Mary and continue to pray before a statue that was one very determined and very loving man's dream.

Francis Cardinal George, OMI
Archbishop of Chicago

Francis Cardinal George, OMI
Archbishop of Chicago

Carl and His Dream

Carl Demma was raised in a traditional Catholic neighborhood in Chicago, where his parish school, All Saints Catholic School, was taught by sisters. On Sunday the collection plate grew heavy with coins, not paper. Boys ran errands for the sisters and sometimes were allowed to miss a day of school to tag along with the priests. Like many young boys, nine-year-old Carl Demma devised various strategies for skipping school for a day.

On one memorable Monday morning, he accompanied his pastor, Monsignor McGalligan, and Chicago's auxiliary bishop, William Cousins, to a downtown bank to deposit the collection from Sunday's Masses. Carl volunteered to watch the car so they wouldn't get a parking ticket while the priests were transacting business inside the bank.

It was an oppressively hot day. Young Carl got out and stood beside the car. When he happened to look up, his eyes became transfixed on a magnificent statue of a woman high atop a tall building. Awed by the sight, he thought, "Oh, God, the Blessed Mother is watching the city!"

When the clergymen returned, they asked what he was staring at. He said, "The Blessed Mother. She is watching the city for us."

The priests explained to him that this was not the Blessed Mother. The building was the Chicago Board of Trade where all of the business for the farmers' products is transacted, and the figure on top of it was Ceres, the Roman goddess of agriculture.

Young Carl found this difficult to believe and, according to his own accounts, became somewhat huffy. He wondered if the priests were playing a joke on him. "Are you sure it's not the Blessed Mother?" he kept asking. Repeatedly, he was assured that it was not.

Young Carl declared, "Then I will build a statue so big that all of Chicago can see her!"

Back at the rectory, the priests frequently joked about "the little guy who is going to build a very big statue." But to young Carl it was not a laughing matter. As he took the streetcar downtown, he frequently saw the statue on top of the Board of Trade building. Repeatedly, he reaffirmed to himself,

"I'm going to build a statue of the Blessed Mother for Chicago. I'm going to do it!"

Cliff Dwellers in Violet and Gold by Michael Cheney

The Early Years

Growing up in the Bridgeport area of Chicago, Carl Demma was the first-generation son of immigrant parents, James and Jennie Demma.

His mother was a devoted churchwoman, and Carl seized every opportunity to be involved with people and activities of the church. As a teenager, he was close to the priests in his parish, a pattern that would continue throughout his life. He mowed the lawn at the church and ran errands for the priests. He and Father Ciezadlo started a teen club that met in the rectory of All Saints Church after school, and Carl helped to plan picnics, trips, and other events for young people. Carl served as an altar boy throughout high school, "long after he was too old to be an altar boy," said one friend.

Known to his friends as Archie, Demma was mischievous and fun loving, always smiling and laughing.

A constant in his life was his devotion to the Blessed Mother. "One day," he recalled, "when I was seven years old, a sister sent me to buy a loaf of bread. At the convent, I saw a life-sized statue of Mary. I could see my aunt and my female cousins in that statue.

"During World War II, I saw the women as pilgrims walking with candles and praying that their sons would come back. I could imagine Mary praying that God wouldn't do this to her son.

"I don't just look at Mary as the Mother of God. She is a special person to me because she is my mother; she's my aunt; she's my cousin; she's my friend. In every woman I've ever come in contact with in my life there's a little bit of Mary.

Young Carl was involved in the activities of his church.

"Through the years, I've turned to the Blessed Mother," Carl said. "I always brought my problems to her, and I've always received an answer from her. She helped me out of the rough spots. There are many mothers in the world, but only one called the 'Mother of God'. That's why I want to bring her to a lot of people."

Another major influence on his young life was his grandmother, who lived nearby. She had twelve children, was a very religious woman, and also very kind. She'd point out the stained glass windows in the church and tell Carl about the lives of the saints.

After he grew up, Carl worked as a truck driver for Signal Delivery. One day, he saw a young lady get off of a bus in his neighborhood. He turned to his fellow driver and said, "I'm going to marry that girl!"

While he was delivering in her area one day, he asked her for a date. She accepted, and he took her to Soldier Field to watch the stock car races. Six years later they were wed. Francine DiGiacomo was twenty-two; he was twenty-five.

The Demmas had two daughters, both of whom developed a rare blood disorder called thalassemia. Carla died when she was eight years old; Judi lived to be twenty-four. Francine said it was their deep faith that sustained them in their sorrow.

Carl and Francine on their wedding day.

Francine added, "Carl was a hard-working, kind, and very generous man. When I was dating him, he gave most of his paycheck to his parents. Even after we were married, if the family needed help – like a refrigerator or a television set – he would buy it for them.

"Everyone who ever met Carl was aware there was something special about him – his goodness, his genuineness."

Carl worked as an insurance salesman for Metropolitan Life Insurance Company for a number of years. In 1961, he opened his own business, Liquorama, in Brighton Park, Illinois. In 1979 he and his partners opened another store, Orland Liquors in Orland Park, Illinois.

Though he no longer mowed the church lawn, he remained dedicated to helping religious institutions. He could be counted on to furnish rides for sisters or, if he was busy, to hire a limousine to take them where they needed to go.

Carla, left, and Judi, right, at their first communions.

Throughout his life, he supported organizations like the Blue Army and was very close to the Sisters of Missionaries of Charity led by Mother Teresa of Calcutta. Mother Teresa once took off the small medal of Mary around her neck and handed it to him.

When he heard that a group of Polish seminarians had no transportation, he bought them a brand-new van. Well known in the community for his generosity, Carl Demma supported school fundraisers and many charitable organizations. He was a member of the Order of the Sons of Italy and the Blue Army of Our Lady of Fatima.

Carl supported Misericordia, a Catholic charity that operates a home for mentally and physically disabled children, and he helped many other religious organizations. He and Francine have hosted exchange students from Italy and Spain.

"Carl was not a holier-than-thou type of guy," said his sister, Antoinette, "but if given the opportunity, he could convert you in an hour."

Carl did not drink alcohol. He told his longtime friend, Father Tony Markus, that he had learned a lot about how sin entered the world. Markus described Carl Demma as a very honest person with a lot of street smarts. Carl said this was part of the reason he was putting most of his earnings toward the statue. He hoped – and believed – the statue would inspire devotion in the faithless and strengthen it in the pious.

He wore his faith like a tattoo. It was etched into him, permanent, apparent, begging for questions, a conversation starter. He talked to Tony Markus about some of the places he could have made choices that were not what God wanted and said he felt God and Mary had saved him. "Remember, you can fool people," Carl said, "but you're always accountable to God. You can't fool Him."

He filled the shelves behind his store counter with religious iconography – plaster figurines, wood carvings, holy pictures. Friend Carmen Schifano carved miniature Jesus heads out of large olive pits, and Carl sometimes handed them out. Carl would occasionally pester him for more heads. Carmen would ask what happened to the one he'd just given him. Carl would reply, "I gave it away. I had to. The Holy Spirit."

Carl didn't feel right unless his day began by receiving the Lord. Rising before dawn, he attended Mass every day at 6:30 a.m., even on vacations. "It's as though it was etched in his heart," said Francine, referring to Carl's need to attend Mass.

Carl didn't just attend Mass; he absorbed it. Often, he would challenge others by asking not only if they had heard the gospel of the day, but what they thought about it. He was never afraid to speak God's word and expressed his thoughts freely.

Carl befriended priests and knew bishops. Pope John Paul II and Joseph Cardinal Bernardin gave him the rosaries he kept in his pocket. On occasion, he stopped by the archdiocese unannounced to bend the cardinal's ear.

The Queen of Peace

On one unforgettable day in 1982, the Demmas' daughter, Judi, told her father about a large and beautiful statue she and her mother had seen at Quigley Preparatory Seminary South (later St. Rita High School). The thirty-two foot statue of the Madonna had been commissioned by Father Sweeney of Our Lady of Peace Catholic Church in Santa Clara, California, and it was on its way there from the artist's studio in Delaware, but its permanent home in California was not yet ready to receive it. A group of Chicago area Catholics had taken advantage of the opportunity to secure the statue for several months until it could travel to its final destination.

Carl returned with Judi to view the statue at Quigley. He later said, "It was unreal – the rosaries, the flowers, and the petitions that were attached to the statue. Clearly, this was having a real impact on the people in that area. "

Suddenly the dream he'd held in his heart for so many years took on a shape he could see and feel. He knew how he would fulfill the vow he had made many years before. He would build a statue just as tall and just as beautiful, but it would be able to travel around to various parishes in the archdiocese.

"This is what Daddy is meant to do," he said to Judi. "This is what God wants from me. I don't know how I'll do it, but I'll do it!"

Young Judi scoffed, "Oh, Daddy, so big? Pu-l-e-e-ze!" She was just the first of many people who respected his devotion but found it difficult to envision the immensity of his dream and the depth of his determination.

One friend to whom Carl talked about his vision was Father Tony Markus, who was, at that time, at Holy Redeemer Church. Fr. Markus said, "I could see putting a large statue in the inner city. You need something larger than life, something that makes you feel the problems of the world can be solved by something bigger than yourself, as God is bigger."

One of Carl's main concerns was young people. "There are so many pressures and bad things going on," he said. "I want to show them that there's a bigger world out there – that Mary, the Mother of Jesus, does care about them. She's a mother to everyone. She can comfort you. God's presence is everywhere."

Carl talked to Tony Markus about how much the statue was going to cost, how he would get the money, where it would go, and how it would be transported.

Carl Contacts Charles Parks

Carl Demma never swerved from the path to the realization of his dream. He asked friends and Marian coworkers, "What do you think of the idea of a big statue that would be mounted on a truck so it could travel to various churchyards and be raised for novenas?" Generally his listeners were polite, but often they were puzzled. Carl's imagination soared to heights that were difficult for others to follow.

One day, Bishop Alfred Abramowicz, who resided at nearby Five Holy Martyrs Church, walked into the store. Carl donated altar wines to the church and supported its fundraisers, and they had become good friends. Carl asked if the bishop had seen the huge statue at Quigley. "Yes," replied Bishop Abramowicz, "I was instrumental in bringing it here."

Immediately, Carl asked the bishop, "How can I get hold of this sculptor? I want to find out how I can make one for Chicago." Bishop Abramowicz replied, "Carl, it's a lot of money; I don't think you can afford it."

"You just tell me," said Demma.

The bishop gave him the name and telephone number of the sculptor, Charles Cropper Parks of Wilmington, Delaware. Carl called Parks and explained that he had seen the Queen of Peace, and he would like the sculptor to make another statue of Mary for Chicago. Carl said, "Society honors its war heroes, its athletes and politicians. They build statues to them, and even though they may be worthy of the honor, there is no one as worthy as Mary."

After several conversations, Carl was unable to convince Parks to take on this project. Carl decided to go to Wilmington to talk to Parks in person, but Parks still refused. "When I asked why he wouldn't build this statue for me," related Carl, "he said lay people just don't do things like this."

Parks explained, "I told Carl I was a bronze man. A project like this is a tremendous amount of work, and I just didn't want to do a second statue of this size."

Carl was devastated.

Clearly, his only choice was to turn to God. He went to St. Anthony's Church in Wilmington and began to pray out loud. "You put this idea in my heart," he admonished the Lord. "Why can't I do it now? Give me a chance. I know I can fulfill this dream I have."

A priest, Father Roberto Balducelli, heard Carl and inquired, "Who are you talking to?" Carl explained his problem and asked the priest whether he thought a large statue of Mary would provide inspiration to people. Father Balducelli believed that, indeed, it would. He added, "Works of art are necessary for the human spirit."

Trying to determine whether Carl had thought through the practicalities of his dream, he asked many questions. Had Carl talked to the bishop in Chicago? Was there a place for the statue? Carl replied that, indeed, he had talked to Cardinal Bernardin and explained his dream and his determination.

Father Roberto became convinced of his sincerity and agreed that this was a worthwhile endeavor. He happened to know the sculptor, and he would contact Parks on Carl's behalf. He explained to Parks that he felt Carl was very serious about this project, and the sculptor agreed to meet with Demma. Carl told the artist the story of his childhood vision and that he was determined to bring a madonna to Chicago. Initially, he called her "Chicago's Lady of Fatima," and then "Our Lady of Chicago" until she was later named "Our Lady of the New Millennium" by the cardinal.

He talked about how important Mary had always been in his life and in the life of his wife and family, but said he believed that

Carl shares his dream with Father Roberto Balducelli and Charles Parks.

children of today were no longer being brought up to revere Mary, that the Church, since the 1960s, was drifting into secularism.

He knew kids wanted to be entertained, and he thought an image of Mary – the bigger, the better – would make a powerful impression on present and future generations of young people.

Carl assured Parks he was really determined to have the statue constructed. Moved by Carl's piety, the artist finally agreed to work with him. Carl asked him how much it would cost. He would prepare to pay for it. They agreed on a price, and Carl said, "Let's start." Parks set out to make a work of art worthy of the kind of devotion he saw in Carl.

Always supportive of Carl's dreams, Francine admits she did ask once, "Does it have to be so big? Wouldn't it be easier to transport if it were smaller?"

But Carl knew the work had to be of remarkable dimensions in order to have the impact he sought for it.

After receiving a payment from Carl, the sculptor made a three-foot model of Mary in clay and resin reinforced with fiberglass. This model resides in a place of honor in the Demma's home today.

After a design was selected, Parks commenced to replicate it in a ten-foot model. (See chapter – The Statue Becomes a Reality – Inch by Inch). Carl would send the artist a little money at a time, and Parks would work on the project as the money came in. Sometimes Parks would wonder whether he was going to be paid for his work. Then Carl would send him a few thousand dollars, and the artist would continue as far as that amount would take him. However, after this larger model was completed, Carl came to the end of his resources.

Francine Demma recalled, "He would talk to everyone he met about it. Sometimes I wondered if he should go on and on about it, but he was a good storyteller, and they would listen. It just amazed me."

Some gave small donations, but it soon became apparent that Carl and Fran would have to fund the statue themselves. They felt that if the project was not successful in the end, it would be impossible to return the money to the donors. Also, Carl had a clear vision of what the statue should be and didn't want others to interfere with his dream based on their donations.

Father Markus said, "Some people felt they wanted to contribute money, some wanting to give a substantial amount, and people would come into his store offering money. But Carl was determined to keep control so his madonna would be able to reach people in the way he envisioned. He didn't want to have to contend with others who could detract from his focus, so he decided to go it alone in regard to financing."

However, he did take one memorable donation. He was visiting two sisters, one of whom was blind. He told her of his mission. She reached into her purse and handed him four pennies, saying, "I know you're going to build a statue of the Blessed Mother, and I want to give this to you for the statue."

So Many Obstacles

There followed a number of years that sorely tested the faith of even such a man as Carl Demma.

He said, "When I'd get close, I'd hit a wall. I was sued, robbed, my children died, and one door after another closed. I was burning with desire, and I was nervous about completing this. At the same time, I knew there was no way I could fail."

To his friend, Carmelo (also known as Carmen) Schifano, he said, "That guy upstairs – you don't know what he puts me through! But I gotta do it. I gotta do it!"

A couple of years into the project, the Demmas' second daughter, Judi, fell victim to the same severe blood disorder that had taken her sister, Carla, at the age of eight. When she was very ill in the hospital, Parks shipped the three-foot model to the Demmas. The resin figure was brown, and Carmen sprayed it silver to replicate the feeling of steel. Carl rolled the fiberglass model down the hall to her room on a hospital cart. It gave comfort to the whole family at a most difficult time.

Judi died at the age of twenty-four and a half, but Carl didn't forget his dream. The Demmas' faith carried them through this terrible time, and even at Judi's funeral, Carl talked to people about the statue and his dream.

However, he sometimes found it hard to discuss his commitment with others. "You can't confide in people because they think you're a kook," he said. "Most of my friends say, 'I couldn't give up that kind of money.'"

Schifano would often chide Carl, "Where's the statue?" Schifano reports, "For years he didn't do anything. He was responsible for a number of people and was going through a lot of personal issues."

Carl would assure his friend that, although his life had taken some detours and he had come up against numerous hurdles, he was going to complete the statue before he died.

Carl's health was a continuing concern. For many years, he had faced numerous physical challenges. He suffered from a mild form of thalassemia, the disease that had taken the lives of his two daughters, and he required many transfusions. He also had hepatitis C, contracted years earlier during open heart surgery, and he had problems with his liver and pancreas. He was also told that he needed another heart operation, but his many other ailments prevented him from being a candidate.

When he went to the doctor, he would say, "You have to keep me going until I finish this!"

However, Demma was always rejuvenated when he thought about the statue and his goal.

After ten years, Schifano continued to ask, "When are you going to do it, Carl?" and Demma would answer, "Before I die."

It finally came to Carl that he wasn't going to be able to pay for Parks to complete the statue unless he took drastic measures. Carl's beloved grandmother had told him, "If you appeal to St. Anthony on his feast day, the saint won't let you down." The Demmas decided to travel to Padua, Italy, to visit St. Anthony's Basilica on the saint's feast day.

The church was packed that day, inside and out, with many others presenting their own petitions. By his own account, Carl found himself actually screaming at the top of his lungs and pleading with St. Anthony or, according to his own words, raving like a maniac. "I've never asked for favors; I've never asked for things in my life," he shouted, "but I really need a favor this time. Let me do it. I know I can do it. I can help the people of Chicago!"

He was interrupted by a member of the clergy who asked, "Who are you talking to? I've never heard anyone talk to St. Anthony that way." In his frustration, Carl answered, "He has to hear my voice!"

And then it hit him like a bomb. "St. Anthony told me in so many words, 'Okay big shot, put your money where your mouth is. Sell your business. Build the statue.'"

This was a life-altering decision. For thirty-five years, Carl had worked to build his business. The Brighton Park store was the Demmas' cushion for retirement. However, he had asked St. Anthony for an answer, and he had gotten one.

Carl told Francine, "I'm going to do it. I don't know how I'm going to do it, but I think I'm going to have to sell my business to get the money."

Schifano reports, "There came a time when Carl turned a corner, and he got a lot of obstacles out of his way. Then it all happened. He sold Liquorama and started showing me pictures from Mr. Parks of a ten-foot prototype. After he sold the store, it cut his workload in half, so he had more time.

"Finally, I said to him, 'You aren't kidding, are you, Carl!' I can hardly believe Carl really did it. The size of it – and the beauty – it's awesome!"

When Charles Parks picked up the phone one day, he was amazed to hear Carl's voice after seven long years. "I thought he might have died," said Parks. But in 1997, Carl told him, "I'm ready to go."

More Obstacles and Hurdles

Finances weren't the only obstacles and frustrations besieging Carl Demma. From the beginning, he sought the counsel and blessings of Catholic leaders, including Mother Teresa, Joseph Cardinal Bernardin, and numerous priests and bishops

At first, Cardinal Bernardin was not supportive, but Carl reminded the cardinal of John 12:8: "The poor will always be with you." He said to the cardinal, "We revere statues of Lincoln and Washington in our country. Why not Mary? Her image has lasted two thousand years. She's a symbol of hope."

In a letter to Carl on December 18, 1985, Cardinal Bernardin wrote:

I have reflected on your plan to commission a 33-foot statue of the Blessed Mother, which would be transported to various parishes and institutions over a period of two years before being placed in a permanent location. You showed me the design of the statue, and indicated what it would cost. Specifically, you asked for my blessing on this venture.

After prayerful consideration and consultation with my auxiliary bishops, I have concluded that I should not support this particular project. At a time when there is so much human need, I find it difficult to endorse the commissioning of a statue that would cost so much. It would be much better to establish an endowment with the money (which could be named in honor of the Blessed Mother), whose annual income could be used for scholarships for needy children, help for the aged, etc. This would, in effect, become a "living statue" which could continue to do good, while at the same time honoring the Blessed Virgin Mary, year after year.

Others reminded Carl how many tuitions his money would pay.

A priest who was a close friend of Carl's, observed, "In the fifteenth century, during the Reformation, people destroyed their statues and stained glass windows. They didn't feel people needed visuals. That isn't true. Beautiful works speak to people. Sometimes the priests forget to listen to the people and what they want.

"After Vatican II, some older clergy felt they were called to get rid of trappings. I don't think that's what it was about. I think it meant we needed to clean out what was inside of us. But it's easier to clean out a room than to clean out what you have inside."

A friend said, "He gave you the feeling that you were with someone who had weathered all kinds of storms and still had hope and faith. When I was with him, I always had a sense of comfort, knowing no matter how bad things got, there was still a feeling of hope.

"He was a big man, and his statue was big. I had a sense of physical presence, a sense of someone who had solidity. He brought a sense of comfort to me."

A Promise from the Pope

As work proceeded, it became increasingly important to Carl that the statue be blessed by the Pope.

In 1998, Francine found a brochure about a pilgrimage that included a visit to Medjugorje and to Rome. At Medjugorje, the Demmas fell in love with the country and the people.

Continuing to Rome, they participated in a general audience with Pope John Paul II in St. Peter's Square. Their friend, Bishop Abramowicz, was a close friend of the Pope. He had arranged for them to have a private audience with the Holy Father. The Demmas waited at their hotel for the phone call telling them of the date and time.

When the call didn't come for several days, they prepared to leave for Florence. Then the phone rang, and a Vatican representative advised the Demmas they would have a private audience the following morning.

With thirty-five other people, Carl and Francine participated in a Mass celebrated by the Holy Father in his private chapel. Afterwards, each member of the group was introduced to the Pope and received a rosary from him.

In his turn, Carl showed the Pope a book with pictures of the statue under construction. The Holy Father had already been told about the statue by Bishop Abramowicz. At first the Pope was a little confused and thought Carl was the artist. However, he soon understood that Carl was the man commissioning the statue.

Then Carl asked the Holy Father if, when it was completed, he would bless the statue. The Pope replied, "If you bring it to me, I will bless it."

Carl presents the statue plan to Pope John Paul II.

The Artist

Born in 1922, Charles Cropper Parks grew up in Wilmington, Delaware, near the Brandywine School of painters. As early as the age of eight, he was carving figures out of soap and soon was whittling wood and modeling clay.

Teachers who saw his drawings encouraged him. In sixth grade, his teachers put him in a separate class. Every day after he completed his homework, he worked on a painting of Horatio at the Bridge, a mural that ran the whole length of the room.

Parks would later draw heavily on the experience he received working in his grandfather's machine shop where his father also worked, and then in a large DuPont industrial plant. He enlisted in the U.S. Air Corps in World War II and became a P-47 fighter pilot.

After the war, Charles Parks enrolled in the University of Delaware where he studied chemical engineering until a professor asked him what he really wanted to do with his life. He realized he wanted to be a sculptor and switched to fine arts.

For four years, he worked in the machine shop during the day and on his sculpture at night. In 1948, he began four years of study at the Pennsylvania Academy of Fine Arts.

In the early fifties, Parks was commissioned to do a mahogany wood carving of the Great Seal of Delaware, as well as a set of aluminum doors for the First Unitarian Church, and a bronze statue for Randolph Macon Women's College in Lynchburg, Virginia. However, national recognition eluded him, and he was forced to maintain his position as foreman at Cropper Machine Company during the day and work on his sculpture at night. He values his experience in the machine shop because he learned technical aspects of his art that sculptors usually have to learn through other avenues. "My grandfather was the best teacher in the world," he declares.

Charles Parks with some of his creations.

Parks and his wife, Inge, and their first child lived in Elsmere, Delaware, where the artist built their home completely out of steel paneling. "It was the cheapest thing available," he said. "I drove every nail in the place. Nearly everything I've done has added to my ability to use different materials."

Always more interested in doing things than in watching others do them, he took voice lessons for ten years and joined Inge in performing in the theater. He would go from work to a performance, then back to work. He was also an accomplished figure skater.

"At least once a year, I'd feel like I had to go out and get another job in order to support the family. A sculptor is like any small business -- the most serious problem is the cash flow," he observed.

After the family moved to Landenberg, Pennsylvania, Parks received occasional commissions, but he decided sculpting was not providing enough money to support his family. Just then, he received a church commission to do a fifteen-foot cruciform statue of Joseph of Arimathea holding the body of Christ. Other commissions followed, including some from foreign countries.

In 1977, the Parks' moved their home and his studio in Wilmington to the banks of the Brandywine River, for which he has always felt a great affinity.

In the 1980s, the artist received a grant from a local philanthropist, so the Parks family, including a daughter and three sons, moved to Greece for a year. While living in Rhodes and on the small island of Simi, Parks became immersed in the world of Greek classic art. The experience awakened a fresh energy in his work as he explored stone carving. When he returned to the U.S., his sculpture began to find the appreciation of a larger audience.

For Parks, the human figure is the most durable and universally understood symbol for the communication of ideas. He has said, "The sculpted human figure is like theater. People will always respond to it with some sort of emotion, be it laughter, tears, a smile, frustration or anger. This is so important to the figurative sculptor. The artwork must say something."

He works on many religious subjects, finding his faith in creation. "Sculpture is my vocation," he said, "and I can't imagine feeling any more religious than when I am looking at a child's head. It takes my breath away. Creation itself is so wonderful, and to perceive it is a religious experience."

Charles Cropper Parks has created more than five hundred sculptures in a wide range of media, including bronze, wood, welded steel, plaster, iron, terra cotta and fiberglass. Since 1977, he has maintained his studio in Wilmington, overlooking the Brandywine River.

Now one of the nation's most respected and prolific sculptors, he has been included in several top art organizations, such as Allied Artists of America, National Academy of Design, and American Artists Professional League. For two years, he served as president of the National Sculpture Society, and he has served on the President's Advisory Committee on the Fine Arts for the John F. Kennedy Center.

The Statue Becomes a Reality-Inch by Inch

In 1986, Parks' first step was to create a three-foot clay model. There were many considerations in regard to the eyes, hair, hands, size, posture, dress, and more. "I wanted her to be different; not to resemble any other statues or portraits of Our Lady," Demma said. "She had to be totally unique. "I also wanted her bigger, so she would have a real impact on people."

When Carl had selected a model for the final design, the artist created a rubber mold that was a negative of the three-foot model. Then Parks created a polyester resin with fiberglass reinforcement to replicate the clay figure in a more durable material.

The completed first section.

After the three-foot fiberglass model was completed, Parks used an instrument called a pantograph. This is a bar with a raised pointer on each end. By running the smaller of the pointers over the three-foot resin

The pantograph in use to construct the second section of the statue.

model, the larger pointer on the other end carved a larger piece of clay to form an identical ten-foot clay enlargement. Then this was modeled to make it perfect, and another rubber mold was made. A resin model, reinforced with fiberglass, was made from this mold.

At this point, the project was put aside. Parks did not hear from Carl Demma for seven years.

When work began again, the ultimate goal was to create a thirty-three-foot work modeled after the ten-foot statue. This time, the artist used a pantograph similar to the one he had previously used, but of much larger scale. He constructed this instrument from two tables connected with a bicycle chain. Parks had never before used this enlargement process for stainless steel and was anxious to find out whether it would work.

He hired an assistant, Matt Large, to create the armature that would be the skeleton of the structure, offering stability for the entire edifice. Three-inch stainless steel tubing was welded horizontally and vertically, with one-inch tubing welded diagonally for wind bracing. Large employed the larger pantograph to determine the points at which the armature would be welded to the statue.

Charles Parks sculpted the face, hands, and feet using the pantograph to enlarge them to the appropriate size for the thirty-three-foot statue.

Parks adapted and broadened the facial design he had used for the Queen of Peace to achieve greater strength and maturity in the delicate face.

The long, graceful hands are nearly clasped in prayer, while Our Lady looks past her hands to the viewer for whom she is clearly praying.

Charles Parks' years in his grandfather's machine shop had given him the understanding of metals and their potential that enabled him to devise a technique for the madonna's robes. Although constructed of stainless steel, she would appear to be made of light. In his mind was the vision at Fatima.

He decided that only stainless steel would withstand rust and

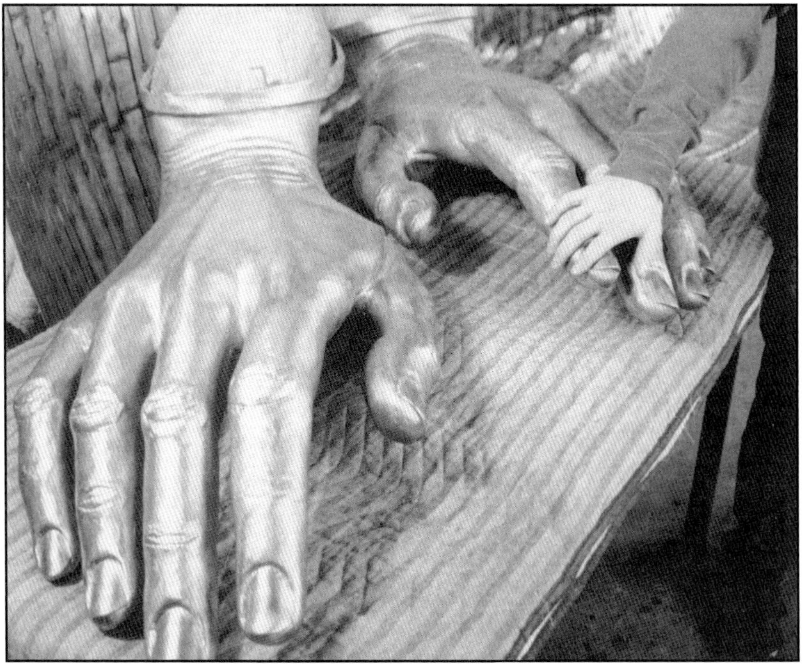

Matt Large holds the hands of Our Lady.

be as durable as he desired. Parks chose to use vertical strips of steel welded together, but with spaces between the strips. With the sheen of the metal, this would achieve the effect of delicate, shimmering ribbons in the long, flowing robes. "You can't light it poorly," he said. It would also allow adequate drainage.

Parks began the garments by obtaining four-by-eight-foot sheets of stainless steel. These were sent to Bruce Industrial in Wilmington to be sheared into strips one-half, one, two, and three inches wide, with some being pointed at the ends. Because of the size of the final piece and the lack of headroom in Parks' studio, the statue was constructed in four sections. The armature was also done in four sections. For the robes, Large welded the stainless steel strips on the quarter sections, one strip at a time, with little weld tacks, a tremendously tedious and time-consuming process.

Parks said of Demma, "I've never dealt with anyone who, once he got going, was so single directed. Carl wanted to know everything that was going on, and he wanted lots of pictures of the project. He talked about little else."

Carl made numerous trips to Parks' studio, sometimes accompanied by Francine, and Parks frequently sent him pictures. Carl said, "Every time I saw a completed section, I was in awe."

Matt Large recalled, "All he could think of was honoring Mary with this thirty-three-foot sculpture. Every time I saw him, he told me he felt it was a way to teach children about Mary."

Because it wasn't possible to assemble the thirty-three-foot statue in the studio, Parks had one wall of his studio taken down in order to take the four completed pieces outdoors. Crowds began congregating to watch Parks and Large at work, and soon traffic became a problem in the small court in which Parks' studio is located.

Gary Johnston of Bruce Industrial used a crane to load the four sections onto his trucks to transport them to his facility. Located in an industrial area, the company had a large, fenced yard. Spectators were allowed to enter and watch during the day, but the gates were closed when work ended in the evening. Johnston said, "It was like a magnet. I've never seen anything draw people like the statue did."

At Bruce Industrial, the two top parts were welded together indoors and then the two lower parts. Security was greatly heightened at the company as each day the crowds of people coming to watch the madonna grew.

Meanwhile, Carl Demma was wrestling with the problem of transporting the statue to Rome for the Pope's blessing. He received estimates approaching $500,000 for transportation each way. One day Francine saw an article in a newspaper saying that His Holiness was scheduling a visit to Mexico and would also stop in St. Louis. If they could have the statue blessed in St. Louis rather than having to take her to Rome, it would be a wonderful solution to a big problem. But would Our Lady be ready by then?

Demma pressured Parks to finish the statue so it could be taken to St. Louis for the Holy Father to bless. The original projection of eighteen months for the welding process was shortened to ten months. For the last several months, Large was spending seventy and eighty-hour weeks on the welding, both inside and outside of the statue.

For the final step, the two large pieces were taken outdoors, and an industrial crane was used to lift the top half of the statue onto the bottom half so it could be connected. There was no time to lose; even though winds and snow swirled around the workers in a Delaware blizzard.

Despite the extraordinary effort of the artist and his assistant, a few details on the draperies were unfinished when time ran out, but it had to be shipped to St. Louis as it was.

Johnston designed and built a structure to protect the statue from vibrations and potholes on the road and to facilitate the lifting process. He constructed it on a flatbed truck that is still in use today. He said, "It would have been easiest to put a sling around the statue's neck, but this would have been upsetting to some of the faithful. A number of priests had conferred with Parks about the handling of the first statue, the Queen of Peace, so we were very sensitive to people's issues. For that reason, it was always hauled with the face up. Although there were sensitivities, we had no problem. Our business is hauling large things."

Our Lady of the New Millennium was lifted by crane and put on the truck to leave for St. Louis while the artist and his team held their breaths, praying the structure would prove as strong as it was designed to be.

Johnston and his wife, Grace, personally drove the statue from Wilmington to St. Louis. There were numerous restrictions, allowing them to travel only during special hours, and not on nights or weekends. Some towns would only allow passage after midnight, and some wouldn't allow it to pass through town at all. It wasn't possible to take the shortest, quickest route because they were not allowed to transport the statue on some roads at all.

However, some of the officials' concerns about the statue's transit seemed justified. As the flatbed carrying the statue drove along the highway, Our Lady of the New Millennium often slowed traffic and drew comments from drivers.

Parks drove separately with Large and another assistant, Erica Johnson.

Pilgrimage to St. Louis

Bishop Abramowicz wrote to Archbishop Justin F. Rigali of St. Louis telling him of the statue and saying it would arrive in St. Louis on January 21, 1999. He assured the Archbishop of Carl Demma's devotion to Mary, the Mother of Jesus Christ, and his desire to take advantage of the Pope's visit to seek the Pope's blessing. He solicited the Archbishop's permission to move it to an appropriate place for the papal blessing.

The Demmas' first destination in St. Louis was Beverage Concept Company, where the owner, Carl's friend Thomas Rand, had agreed to house the statue until a site could be found during the Pope's visit. The Demmas were pleased to find the statue had arrived and was resting on the flatbed truck on which it had traveled from Delaware.

Carl and Francine went to the office of the Cathedral Basilica of St. Louis, hoping to see Archbishop Rigali to obtain his aid. They were told the Archbishop had left for Mexico City to meet the Pope. A sister said that there was nothing she could do to help them find an appropriate site for the statue, and a young priest said the same.

Then, a monsignor ushered the Demmas into his office and told them he had seen pictures of Our Lady of the New Millennium and remembered Carl's request for help in finding a site. He applauded Carl's efforts as "noble" and said he would help if he could. Later that day, the monsignor called the Demmas at their hotel and gave them the number of the local Secret Service office so they could explain their plan.

It was a sensitive time in St. Louis. The most powerful man in the

Raising the statue in St. Louis.

Christian world was arriving in town and was to be greeted at the airport by President Clinton, the most powerful political leader in the world. Security was intense, and anything out of the ordinary was closely scrutinized.

Gary Johnston and Carl drove around St. Louis for a day and a half trying to find a place for the statue. While driving along the route the Pope's motorcade would take, the Demmas noticed a gas station next door to a laundromat. Carl got out of the car and approached the gas station attendant, who told him he must talk to the owner who would be in later.

The Demmas returned to the gas station where the owner, Maria Flora, said she would be honored to have Our Lady placed in the lot of the laundromat. There would be no charge.

Johnston recalls, "She had to shut down the gas pumps because of all the people. But a lot of people went into her store, so I guess it was okay."

When he called the Secret Service number, Carl was told he would have to go to the police station to get a permit. At the police station, a woman police officer told the Demmas that there was nothing that could be done for them. Becoming very annoyed, Francine declared, "We have brought Our Lady from Wilmington, Delaware, and now you're going to refuse us?"

Her challenge brought about a change of heart, and the

woman officer commented that, no matter where the statue was placed, the Pope would bless it because he blessed everything, even the trees. Then she talked to the police captain who said, if the Demmas could find a site, they could proceed. Carl told him they already had a site.

Our Lady leaves viewers breathless as she stands for the very first time.

Shortly after the Demmas returned to their hotel, two Secret Service men came to their room asking where Carl had obtained the statue and where he had gotten the money to build it. Carl shared pictures of Our Lady of the New Millennium and assured them the Pope was aware the statue was going to be in St. Louis. With a smile, Francine joked with the Secret Service men, saying, "You think you have something with your stainless steel arch? Wait until you see Our Lady!"

Carl went to the convention center to pick up Bishop Abramowicz and his sister, Esther, and bring them to the laundromat parking lot. When they returned, the group sang "Happy Birthday" to the bishop on his eightieth birthday in front of Our Lady of the New Millennium.

Charles Parks had arrived in St. Louis with his two assistants, Matt Large and Erica Johnson, and they were on hand when the statue reached the site where it was to be erected.

Carl had previously contacted Frank Smoczynski, a friend

The statue in place in St. Louis.

with whom he had worked on numerous Marian projects and who had been involved in bringing the Queen of Peace statue to Chicago. Carl asked him for help in erecting the statue in St. Louis. Smoczynski, in turn, contacted Terry Doyle of Doyle Sign Company in Addison, Illinois who had also been instrumental in erecting the Queen of Peace in Chicago.

Smoczynski asked if Doyle could work out the details of setting up the statue in St. Louis. Doyle contacted Warren Sign Company in St. Louis to arrange for an industrial crane to raise the statue on its designated site and support it while in St. Louis. Doyle also had a sign made with the name of the statue and had it placed at the foot of the statue.

The truck on which the statue lay was parked behind the building. Those watching held their breath as Warren's industrial crane lifted the statue into the air and lowered it to the ground in the parking lot.

Francine recalls, "It was a cold, windy day. I was standing in the laundromat as I watched the crane raising Our Lady for the first time. As she rose, I noticed the sun pulsating in the sky. I went out to tell Mr. Parks that Our Lord was well pleased. He just smiled."

On January 27, 1999, Pope John Paul II, the first Pope ever to visit St. Louis, spoke to more than one hundred and ten thousand worshippers in the Trans World Dome, a cavernous sports palace and convention center that had been transformed into a cathedral. In his homily, the Pope called for a renewal of faith and a rededication to the sanctity of life. "It must start with families," he said, "the most vital foundation of society, the first school of social virtue and solidarity."

The thousands of faithful who were unable to gain entrance stood up to forty deep along the pontiff's route through the city, hoping to catch a glance of history.

As the Holy Father was being driven from the Culture Center, he looked up, and his car slowed slightly. He looked at Our Lady and made the sign of the cross. This moment of blessing was captured by a Channel 7 film crew, and the moment of joy and triumph for the Demmas was captured on videotape. Carl was wearing a huge smile and breathing a great sigh of relief, bringing chuckles from the people around him.

Gary Johnston observed, "I've never seen anything in my life that could move people like that statue. In St. Louis, I think as many people came to see the statue as to see the Pope.

"People wanted to get close to it and touch it. It was just phenomenal. They wanted to know how it was built and why it

The Pope blessing the statue...

and Carl's reaction.

was built. The 'why' was the hardest to answer. Even the guys who work for me were affected. It changes people's whole attitude. There's just a different feeling when you're around it."

Cherie Ammon of St. Charles, Illinois, was attending the event as a representative of the Queen of the Americas Guild. She watched many cars pulling up to get a closer look at the statue, and Cherie handed out Our Lady of Guadalupe holy cards. "You would have thought I was giving them gold," she said.

"People were approaching the statue, lifting their children up to touch her. Many went across the street to get a better look. They just couldn't leave!"

A man in a small office across the street approached Cherie and said, "I'm not a Catholic but could you pray for me? For some reason, the mother of Jesus is across the street from my business. I don't know what to think of this. She could have been anywhere, but she's parked right in front of my business."

Cherie says, "I could see from his face he was not Catholic, but he really felt the love she has for all of us. He told me he sat out the night before, looking at her in the spotlight – all night."

She recalled a father who came to see the Blessed Mother with a baby in his backpack and another baby in front. The child in back seemed to have Down syndrome. Cherie observed, "Clearly this was a pro-life dad. As he came down the street people cheered for him."

He told Cherie that the little boy's name was John Paul.

Greatly moved, Cherie observed, "There is so much going on in today's world – wars, uncertainty. Then the Holy Father comes to send our young people out to be fishers of men, and here is the Blessed Mother looking at us and holding her hands out to us."

While she stood by Our Lady, Carl told her the story of his sighting Ceres atop the Board of Trade Building. "He was a real storyteller," said Cherie. "How many times had I walked under that building and never made the connection he made, which would one day bring the Mother of God to everyone in

Chicago."

Some priests had brought a group of young children to see the Pope, and they came to see Our Lady. While Carl talked to the children and the priests, a nine-year-old boy named Andrew looked up at Francine and said, "You must be very proud of your husband."

Choked up, she gave him a big hug and thought to herself, "If a child could see what a wonderful accomplishment this is, the whole world should see it!"

The Archdiocese

Carl knew that, in order to fulfill his dream of sharing Our Lady of the New Millennium with the people of Chicago, he would need to work with the Archdiocese of Chicago, and he sought the support of Francis Cardinal George, who had risen to this position after the death of Cardinal Bernardin.

At that time, the Most Reverend Raymond E. Goedert was Vicar General of the Archdiocese of Chicago. One of his functions was to protect the cardinal from being overwhelmed with appointments, and he would frequently refer people to others in the hierarchy who could help them or solve their problems. So when Carl attempted to see the Cardinal, he was advised that he must first make an appointment with Bishop Goedert.

Carl told the bishop the story of his childhood sighting of Ceres and his vow to build a statue of the Blessed Mother for Chicago. He talked about the terrible loss of his daughters.

Bishop Goedert recalls, "I was extremely impressed with his amazing faith, with how he was able to accept the death of his two daughters, and his determination to honor the Blessed Mother. Before we were finished, I felt this was a man the cardinal had to see. It was not so much because Carl needed to see the cardinal as because I got so much out of our conversation.

"Every now and then you come across someone who has such extraordinary faith it moves you. Carl did that for me. I remember telling the cardinal that he had to meet this man." Years later, the Bishop said that he had felt Demma was a man on a mission, and the archdiocese should support him.

But the bishop was concerned about many of the practical situations that would be involved when the statue was raised at a site and when it was transported from one site to another. For instance, something this spectacular, he could see, would automatically attract attention. Drivers would be slowing down their cars to look, causing traffic and safety hazards.

Cardinal George's recollection of his first conversation with Carl Demma was of the man's frustration and fear that his statue would not be accepted. Carl indicated he was having trouble contacting the people who could help him reach other people whose help he needed.

The cardinal talked to Demma about many of the obstacles he was facing, many of them not ecclesiastical. The city as well as the Church would have to agree to his plans.

Carl gained a reputation for devotion and determination – to the point of stubbornness – but he never took his eye off of his goal.

His friend, Peter Coppa, observed, "It was a great spiritual battle between good and evil. There were so many critical decisions to be made and obstacles and setbacks to overcome, and sometimes it was heartbreaking."

Since the statue would be designed to travel to parishes throughout the Chicago area and even beyond, there were questions about liability. Virtually every parish it visited would be archdiocese property. If someone were to get hurt, either moving it or while it was at another location, who would be responsible?

Vital Statistics

Weight - 8,400 pounds
Height – 33 feet, 8 inches
Truck 61 feet long
28 feet wide – when outriggers are out
11 feet wide without outriggers
38 feet from the ground when erect
When down – 13 feet, 16 inches

If the statue were damaged, who would be liable?

Richard Dellacroce, who served as Demma's attorney in his dealings with the archdiocese and the city, reflects, "When you're full of the spirit and are working so hard toward your goal, you feel that others should be welcoming your efforts and making them easy. When you're committed to and wrapped up in a project, you may just see what you want done, but not think of the practical aspects." As an attorney, he understood why the archdiocese required Carl to sign numerous waivers and to obtain very expensive liability insurance. "Carl and I had a meeting with the bishop and the archdiocese's attorneys, and once the insurance was in place, everything flowed smoothly."

But to Fran, it seemed the obstacles would never be overcome. "There were all of these legal people, and they seemed to make it so difficult for him. It often seemed like it was Carl against the world."

Demma said to his friend, "Our Lady will continue to have an impact on people long after I am gone." He was committed to honor not just the Lady, but all mothers.

But Carl could feel time slipping away. He wanted to see the statue finished while he was alive, and he wanted to see the reaction of people to it.

Dellacroce said, "As I look back, I'm very proud of having been an instrument to help in the realization of Carl's dream. When I first saw Our Lady of the New Millennium, I was overwhelmed. I knew everything he had to do to get this done. He was a child of vision and then a man of vision, and he wasn't afraid to work and to sacrifice."

Back to Wilmington

After the Pope's visit, the statue was lifted by crane onto the flatbed truck on which it had traveled, and Gary and Grace Johnston drove it back to Wilmington so that Parks and his staff might complete the work that still needed to be done.

Parks called the Demmas to say that there was going to be a retrospective exhibit of his work in a gallery at the Riverfront Art Center in Wilmington. He asked for the Demmas' permission to display the statue in front of the gallery.

Final work on the statue was completed, and Gary Johnston again transported her and raised her at the gallery site. During a brief ceremony, public officials recognized Charles Parks as the artist who had created the statue and the other work on display in the gallery. Francine recalls, "Then they called out our name – Mr. and Mrs. Carl Demma. We stepped up, and they gave us the key to the city."

From the first day, there was a constant caravan of cars driving by.

Wilmington children in front of the statue.

Numerous Catholic schools in the Wilmington area brought children to see the statue. Demma was enchanted with the

Thank You
Mary
Thank
Statue of
Mary

children, and the children were enchanted with the statue. Carl said to Francine, "I know I did the right thing."

After they returned home, the Demmas received a group of drawings of the statue done by the children of St. Hedwig School with their comments and their thanks to the Demmas for creating the statue.

It became clear that the type of crane used in St. Louis and in Wilmington to raise the statue would be a costly and inconvenient method of erecting the statue at the multiple parishes and locations to which Carl envisioned taking it. Demma asked Johnston to design a mechanism and to retrofit a trailer so the statue could remain fixed to the flatbed for traveling and could be raised and lowered hydraulically.

"I didn't want to take on another time consuming job like this, but Carl was very persuasive in a charmingly exasperating way," said Johnston. "He was the biggest pain I ever met. He never took no for an answer. He told me, 'You're going to have to do it or you adopt me for a son and you'll never get rid of me.'"

Carl described what he had in mind, and Johnston sketched it out. It looked like it would do the job, and Carl agreed to a price.

◂Thank you cards created by the children of
Saint Hedwig School in Wilmington, Delaware.

Our Lady Arrives in Chicago

Michael Tadin, owner of Marina Cartage in Chicago, had been a lifelong friend of Carl and his family. Although Bruce Industrial had constructed the hydraulics and mechanics for the trailer, there was as yet no truck outfitted with a hydraulic system to pull the trailer. Demma contacted Tadin for advice on buying a truck and told him why he needed it. This was the first Tadin had heard about the statue.

He recalls, "When we found out what a wonderful thing he was doing, we offered to let him use one of our trucks and our driver. We told him his money wasn't going to be spent with us! We wanted to be a part of this unbelievable endeavor.

Our Lady arrives at Holy Name Cathedral.

"Many of the people who should be living their faith were not doing it. Here was a man who had so much tragedy and trial in his life. He shouldn't have had such great faith, but he believed when no one else did."

The statue arrived in Chicago on Monday, May 3, 1999, lying on Bruce Industrial's flatbed truck. Gary Johnston of Bruce Industrial, who designed and built the structure on which the statue rested, had also drawn schematics for a hydraulic system to raise and lower the statue on the flatbed truck.

Johnston showed Tadin the type of hydraulics needed by the tractor to operate the mechanism on the flatbed, and Tadin contacted Heil Equipment who immediately got to work to adapt one of Marina's trucks. Heil personnel devised a three-stage hydraulic pump and attached it to Marina's truck, also donating their work and materials. A crane lifted the statue onto the new mechanism and, by Thursday, May 6, the rig and the statue returned to Marina Cartage.

That day, the archdiocese's attorney, with an insurance representative and another representative of the archdiocese, gathered in Marina's parking lot. Our Lady of the New Millennium rose up on her hydraulic lift for the first time. Every person in attendance was stunned by her beauty and power as she stood.

The awestruck archdiocese representatives immediately phoned Bishop Goedert to tell him what they had seen, and he asked them to bring the statue to Holy Name Cathedral immediately.

Mike Tadin had appointed one of his drivers, Tom Brischetto, to drive the truck, accompanied by Marina's shop foreman, John Halpin, to handle the hydraulics. Heil instructed the twosome how to operate the hydraulic mechanism to raise and lower the statue.

Because of regulations forbidding driving this size load at night, the statue was not taken to the cathedral until the next morning. When set up in the parking lot directly across from the cathedral, viewers were again stunned by her amazing beauty and size.

Tom Brischetto said, "We were pretty nervous about driving this statue through the city. With most loads, if you damage the truck or the load, you can take it back to the shop for repair, but not this time. Both the truck and the statue are unique."

When they arrived at the cathedral, they found no way to access the parking lot with this large a truck without driving over some bushes. One of the priests said, "Just go right over the bushes;

we'll replace them if we have to."

Tom recalled, "We went over the bushes, and they popped right back up again. Any other truck would have killed those bushes. Amazing. I asked myself if this had some special meaning."

Tom maneuvered the truck, and John handled the mechanism, stabilizing it and then attaching the hoses to the hydraulic pumps. First it was determined that the site was level. The two dolly legs on the truck were put in place, and outriggers on each side of the center of the trailer were extended to provide stability. Then the hoses for the hydraulic system were attached. The statue was then raised and locked in place, and the cradle that had supported the statue in transit was lowered back down.

Tom said, "It was the first time we had put it up, and it went fine. Right away, the huge statue started getting people's attention. It was pretty exciting."

Carl and Fran were on hand for this milestone moment. Bishop Goedert recalls, "We couldn't imagine what the statue was going to look like, or how they could get it into the city through all of the viaducts and other obstacles. As we saw it coming down State Street on the flatbed, we were amazed at the skill of the driver. He came right in, backed right over the curb and into the parking lot, and placed it where they could elevate the statue."

A Special Mother's Day Celebration

Each year on Mother's Day, Francis Cardinal George celebrated a Mass for expectant mothers. Our Lady of the New Millennium arrived at Holy Name Cathedral the day before this service in 1999.

Carl Demma was anxious to have the Cardinal bless the statue. Cardinal George had inquired, "The Pope has blessed it. Why do you want me to bless it?" Carl replied, "I want you to bless it for the people of Chicago."

After the Mother's Day Mass and presentation of a white silk rose to each expectant mother in the congregation, the Cardinal announced he was going to bless Our Lady of the New Millennium, and he invited everyone to join him. With many of the worshipers following, Cardinal George proceeded across the street where he gave his blessing to Our Lady.

This was the first occasion on which Carl stood near the statue, handing out the cards with the picture of Our Lady of the New Millennium on one side and the Memorare on the other. Throughout the statue's travels, these cards would be provided by Perfect Plastic Printing Corporation.

Cardinal George speaks with Carl.

At this time, the Cardinal also told Carl he was sorry about the obstacles that had been placed in his way by the Archdiocese. He said to Fran, "I believe Carl was directed by God to do this."

Subsequently, Cardinal George made the following statement in the Catholic New World newspaper of the Archdiocese of Chicago:

"On Mother's Day, at Holy Name Cathedral, I blessed a new statue of the Blessed Mother. It is the gift of a man who loves Mary profoundly and who believes that this statue will be the occasion for God to grant many graces to the Archdiocese...

"For all its size, it is graceful and inviting rather than a colossus. Constructed of steel ribbons which allow light to penetrate it, it will be, I hope, a sign of God's light in our lives and be well received in our parishes.

"May we use its visit to ask our Blessed Lady, patroness of the United States of America, to bless our land and all those who make their home here."

The Cardinal apologized to Carl for all of the inconveniences he had experienced and asked Carl to keep in contact with him. "This is what the city needs," said Cardinal George.

Now Our Lady of the New Millennium was ready to begin the odyssey that has touched the lives of so many.

Cardinal George blessing the statue.

An Amazing Response

A letter from Bishop Goedert to Carl Demma on May 21, 1999, congratulated Carl and Francine on the beautiful statue.

In this letter, Bishop Goedert said, "In regard to the holy card, the Cardinal requested that the Blessed Mother's title be Our Lady of the New Millennium. On the reverse side, he would like to have the coat of arms of the Archdiocese along with the Memorare prayer." Carl had decided upon using the Memorare some time before, but had written to Cardinal George for his approval and statue name suggestions.

At that time, the Archdiocese was in the midst of a three-year planning effort for the celebration of the Jubilee Year 2000 in Chicago. The two major events were to be a large celebration called the Way of Faith at Mundelein Seminary and a huge Corpus Christus gathering of the Archdiocese at Soldier Field, the highlight of the Jubilee Year. Other projects included creating an evangelization program and creating a mission band of one hundred preachers and scheduling them for Lenten missions.

Father Wayne Prist, pastor of All Saints Basilica, was in charge of the Archdiocese's celebration of the Jubilee Year. He was assisted by Alejandro Castillo, Director of the Millennium Office. They heard that there was a gentleman who had plans to move a large statue around the Archdiocese of Chicago. Then, all of a sudden, this amazing statue had arrived in the city on a truck, and the Archdiocese wasn't sure exactly what to do with it. Castillo was delegated to be the Archdiocese's representative for all matters regarding the statue.

Since the Cardinal had seen the statue at Holy Name Cathedral, he was anxious to make it a part of the millennium observance, to mark the millennium in a devotional way, and to help refresh love of Blessed Mary in the hearts of the faithful in the Archdiocese. He wanted to make it available to the parishes for their use in this way and gave his permission for the statue to be taken to any parish that requested it.

Al Castillo began getting calls asking where the statue was currently appearing and where it would be going in the future. He initiated a voice mail system at the Archdiocese office to apprise callers of her weekly moves and her schedule for the month.

It was several weeks before he had the opportunity to see the statue himself. Despite reading and hearing much about Our Lady of the New Millennium, he was not prepared for what he saw.

"I was amazed by the sight of her," he said, "and by the people there and the reverence they had for the presence of Our Lady in their midst. I was awed by the silence of the people milling about, all in a prayerful mood.

"I was just stunned when I saw this beautiful work of art."

He recalled thinking about Carl Demma and what an imagination this man had to be able to conceive of this and make it a reality. "Unless you actually see it, you have no idea. Whatever it cost, the time spent on it – not only the statue but the mechanism to raise her up – was beyond my comprehension."

In response to questions from the parishes, Castillo compiled an information sheet that was mailed out to anyone who called with an inquiry. (See box on the following pages.)

Initially, when the parish sign-up forms were being returned, it was clear that there was much more interest than had been anticipated. Castillo asked the Demmas how they would like to proceed.

Since there was an overwhelming number of requests, Castillo and his assistant, Gilda Valentino, began the process of sorting through all of the requests by vicariate and then by proximity to one another. The initial quantity of requests was sufficient to move the statue on a weekly basis during the spring, summer, and fall for three years.

As the waves of calls became an avalanche, Francine Demma took on much of the challenge of working with the Archdiocese in scheduling the statue's visits. As people became aware of the statue, and they heard about Francine, often they would contact her directly. Eventually Francine was scheduling virtually all of the statue's visits, informing the Archdiocese where it would be appearing on what dates.

Castillo recalls, "We also sent out a letter and a form to all of the parishes asking if anyone would be interested in hosting the statue. We expected fifteen or twenty replies. We got well over one hundred and fifty responses.

"Everybody wanted her in May. Of course, we couldn't accommodate that. People would request to have her for a special event at their parish. It sometimes broke my heart when we weren't able to fulfill their wishes.

"This was supposed to be about three percent of my job, but it turned out, at some points, to be fifty percent of the job, with calls coming in from all over. In the three-year period that I was working on the Jubilee celebration, except for the Soldier Field event, this generated by far the most calls from people wanting to know where she was and where she was going. Once people had seen her, the number of calls became even greater."

Groups began holding overnight vigils, waiting for the arrival of the truck on which Our Lady lies during transport.

Castillo said, "We have a significant number of Mexicans and Poles living in this area, and this quickly became an international event."

Immigrant families brought relatives into the country to see the statue. They brought their families and friends who were visiting from their home countries.

It became clear to Al and Francine that the scheduling would have to be done in a more organized way. Initially the statue changed locations every week, and no thought was given to the relative locations to and from which she would move. She might go from a site on the south side of the city to a parish on the north or west side.

The statue was scheduled to go from one location to another that was nearby, rather than traveling all the way across the city or suburbia. With six vicariates in the Archdiocese, it was routed to cover each equitably. Visits were often lengthened to two weeks to reduce the amount of travel. Carl and Francine accompanied the statue to every parish she visited.

To aid each parish in preparing for the visit of Our Lady of the New Millennium, the Archdiocese prepared this helpful information for host parishes.

Based on questions received by the Communications Office from parishes that have hosted the statue in the past, the following Q & A were assembled.

Do we need insurance?

No. A certificate of insurance is on file at the Pastoral Center.

What about lighting?

The statue comes with three spotlights. Some parishes have made arrangements to have additional lights brought in for brighter illumination, but that would be up to the parish's own discretion.

Can the parish take up a collection?

There are no restrictions against parishes selling religious articles. Parishes have sold candles and other items. The Communications Office does not keep vendor lists. Typically, parishes are approached directly from the vendors selling these items. If you are interested in selling a certain item, contact parishes that have sold these items in the past for vendor information.

How do we handle calls regarding the statue?

While the Communications Office will handle many of the calls, host parishes will probably receive their share of calls. Content of the calls will vary. Most people will ask for directions or a schedule of activities, and some people will want to know the statue's arrival and departure times. A recommendation would be to assign an individual prepared with answers to the above questions to answer these calls. When an individual is unavailable to take calls, we recommend that calls go to an answering machine. A volunteer may then be assigned to return selected calls on an hourly basis.

Media

The statue usually makes news whenever she moves. Have a spokesperson ready and able to be interviewed by local media. Submitting a picture and a small story about the experience to the local paper is always a plus. Don't forget to place an invitation and a schedule of services in your upcoming bulletin!

Also, the schedule will be published in the Catholic New World as well as posted on the archdiocesan website www.archchicago.org

What time can we expect the statue to arrive/depart?

The driver and engineer will arrive on Sunday morning between the hours of four a.m. and six a.m. The process takes a little more than half an hour.

Do I need to be present upon its arrival and departure?

Not necessarily. The only request is that the parish leave an indication of the location and direction they wish the statue to face.

Do we need to hire a security guard?

It is not required. However, some parishes have hired a security guard, while others have informed their local police department that the parish would be hosting the statue.

Is it necessary to alert local authorities?

You are not obligated to, but may want to for a few reasons.

As a courtesy: Treat this occasion as you would a large ongoing event that will include many visitors (from all parts of this Archdiocese, neighboring diocese and, in some instances, different parts of the world) to your neighborhood and parish grounds.

Traffic concerns: There will be points throughout the week where you will experience a large number of people driving by and looking for a place to park. Depending on your location this may cause some traffic difficulties.

Safety: The statue will be available for viewing twenty-four hours a day. Some parishes have reported people stopping by at all hours of the night. Asking local police to make a few extra trips by the parish grounds would put people visiting the statue a little more at ease.

What else can a parish do to be better prepared?

Plan to contact or visit the parishes that have recently hosted the statue. You might see something or they may share an experience or two that will make you better prepared and the time with the statue a little more special.

What kinds of accommodations are required for visitors?

As with all of the above, there are no hard and fast rules. Here are a few things parishes have had on hand:

- Tents, especially in the hot summer months
- Water
- Portable toilets
- Chairs

Again, visit/call parishes that have hosted the statue to get a clearer picture beforehand.

When should we schedule prayer services?

The statue has been prone to mechanical problems in the past. Having a prayer service for the statue on the day of its arrival is not recommended. However, if you do have a prayer service on the day of its arrival, make sure you have an alternate prayer service that makes allowances in the event that the statue has not arrived (breakdown en route) or has difficulty being situated (difficulty with the hydraulic system).

The best time would probably be on Monday evening with a large farewell gathering scheduled on Saturday.

The Dream Comes True - Early Visits

Carl Demma thought he would build the statue and perhaps be the only one praying before her. "I thought I would just go to her and say the Rosary, and maybe ten people would show up," he once said.

He looked forward to showing Our Lady of the New Millennium in a few places, hopefully where it would be seen by many children. But, after the blessing of the statue on Mother's Day and the publicity the statue received, word spread quickly.

St. Jerome's Croatian Church

After Mother's Day, Our Lady was returned to Marina Cartage while arrangements were made to transport her to St. Jerome's Croatian Church on the south side of Chicago, her first parish visit. The events there gave a small glimpse into the way she would be received by many in the coming months and years and what she would mean to so many people.

When she arrived at St. Jerome's on May 12, she was given an enthusiastic reception by the people of the community and the two holy parish priests. Carl Demma was jubilant.

The next evening, Carl and Francine attended Mass at St. Jerome's. As they went out to visit Our Lady, an attractive young woman said to Francine, "When I see her, it makes me want to be good." Many said they would like to keep her in their parish.

The Demmas returned to St. Jerome's on Saturday and found two sisters in front of the statue with tears in their eyes. They explained that they had lost their mother a few weeks before, and it was comforting for them to see Our Lady. Francine gave each a prayer card with the Memorare on the back. The sisters said they had always prayed that prayer with their mother. Francine said, "I became very emotional seeing how comforting it was for them just to be there."

At Sunday morning Mass, the priests told the congregation about Carl, and they applauded him for bringing the statue to their parish. A sumptuous feast followed in the school hall.

Our Lady at St. Jerome.

As the Demmas went back to their car, a man walking his dog asked, "Did you see the moon?" Francine looked up and saw one bright star and a sliver of the moon above Our Lady. "It will never leave my mind," said Francine. "The beautiful creation of God!"

On Friday, May 20, Carl and Francine attended Benediction Services and Rosary at St. Jerome's Church. They were told that a man's video camera had been stolen while he went across the street to get a better view of the statue. Two days later the camera, which had been wrapped, was brought back to the rectory.

On Saturday, the Demmas brought their friend, Bishop Abramowicz, to see Our Lady, and he was delighted at the reception she was receiving. Two brides and their bridal parties had pictures taken in front of the statue of the Blessed Mother. The bishop was amazed at the number of people who would stop their cars and make the sign of the cross. Others came up to the bishop and said they had been confirmed by him.

Smiling like a proud father, Carl Demma happily handed out holy cards and talked to parishioners. He was especially delighted to talk to the children.

St. Germaine

The second parish visited by Our Lady of the New Millennium was St. Germaine, the Demmas' home parish.

Moonbeams Light Our Lady at St. Germaine.

Although Carl had often talked to Father Robert Malloy about the building of the statue, the priest really didn't know what to expect when it arrived at St. Germaine for the first time. Little preparation was made for her arrival.

Father Malloy commented, "I had no idea how people would react. When the statue was raised, we were amazed!

"People were awestruck by what they saw. Because of her size, she was visible for a long distance, and word of her arrival spread like crazy throughout the whole South Side of Chicago. We began getting all kinds of visits from our parishioners and others.

"I saw the people start coming to look at her, so we thought we ought to set out some chairs. Then we set out more chairs. People were bringing flowers, so we put out some tables. Soon there were over fifty bouquets. Then they brought donations, so we put boxes out.

"We saw some people were going to stay through the night, so we put on some lights.

"People were asking many questions about her, so we made up a little brochure about her history. We decided to have some prayer services and prayed the Rosary.

"It was very haphazard and spontaneous, and we just learned from our experience. The second time she visited us, we were better prepared."

Francine Demma recalled, "The second night after she arrived, we began saying a Rosary every night at seven p.m. Another group would say the Rosary at nine a.m. It was wonderful for the people of our parish to join together as a community in prayer."

On the evening of Memorial Day, it rained all afternoon. It was decided to have the evening Rosary in the church, but Francine suggested waiting. Around 6:45 p.m., someone came up to her and asked, "Did you see the rainbow?" Francine rose from her chair, went outside, and looked at the sky where there was a rainbow centered over Our Lady. Francine said, "Actually, there was a second, fainter rainbow. That is the first time in my life I have ever seen a double rainbow."

Marita McKenna recalls, "When I arrived at St. Germaine, there were only about six of us. A dark storm was brewing as we prayed the Rosary. All of a sudden, there was a huge flash of lightning that looked like it hit the statue, and a clap of thunder so loud we all cringed and screamed. Then, to our amazement, the clouds parted and a triple rainbow was radiantly framed over Our Blessed Mother. It was the most beautiful visit I have ever had with the Blessed Mother."

On another evening, a man gave Francine a photograph he had taken of Our Lady. In the light of the setting sun, she appeared to be made of solid gold.

Passing out palm-sized holy cards at the back of the church parking lot, pausing occasionally to gaze up at Our Lady of the New Millennium or to accept a compliment from visitors, Carl Demma was described as the epitome of the modest Everyman. A small smile would break out on his face as he surveyed groups of people coming together in reverence, humbly reaching out for a small bit of grace.

"I think I've done something constructive with my life," he said.

The mood of the people was reflected as their references to the statue became "she" and "her" rather than "it."

The Shrine of Pompeii

In the environment of an Italian culture, the people at the Shrine of Pompeii were moved to express their devotion and affection for Our Lady of the New Millennium in a new way. As Italians, they felt the statue needed to be dressed, but she was too large for the beautiful mantle they wanted to give her.

So they decided to make her a crown.

After seeking the Demmas' permission, they had a professional florist create a crown of flowers proportionate to the huge figure. A cherry picker lift was used to place it upon her head, the first time the statue had been decked in this manner.

The crowning of Our Lady at the Shrine of Pompeii.

Then some reflected that images of the Madonna are often shown holding a rosary. The florist was asked to create a gigantic rosary of flowers, and this was placed in her hands.

Father Richard Fragomeni, Professor of Liturgy and Preaching at the Catholic Theological Union of Chicago, and Rector at the Shrine, observed, "Catholicism as a religion has a unique core called 'sacramentality' meaning created things such as bread, wine, and oil, through which we can actually come to know God. It comes from the strong Catholic belief in the incarnation. So many human experiences become encounters with God."

"The other side is the danger of idolatry. I am sure this image could be seen by some as an idol -- Catholics worshiping stainless steel. This could be happening in some cases, but I believe there is something deeper going on. I sense that this statue, like other images we create, is a window through which we begin to get a glimpse of the presence of God and, in this case, the affectionate care of the Mother."

"In a piece of art like Our Lady of the New Millennium, the first impact is daunting. The second impact is in the life of people who are touched and go away changed, inspired to live a better life."

The Way of Faith

The first of the two major celebrations of the Archdiocese of Chicago for the Jubilee Year 2000 was the Way of Faith on the grounds of Mundelein Seminary at the University of St. Mary of the Lake in Mundelein, Illinois. The Archdiocese of Chicago was anxious for Our Lady of the New Millennium to be a part of this celebration.

On September 16 and 17, over two glorious early autumn days, thousands of Catholics took a three-mile walk back in time to relive the history of the Catholic Church in Chicago.

Cardinal George and several auxiliary bishops led participants on a historical pilgrimage through thirteen "stations" that depicted pivotal moments in the history of nearly one hundred and sixty years of the local Catholic Church.

Area parishioners donned costumes to represent famous Catholics - Pere Jacques Marquette, St. Frances Cabrini, and others ~ whose lives the pilgrimage honored.

Participants concluded their pilgrimage at the north end of the campus near the 33-foot-tall statue which was placed where she could bestow welcome on all those completing the walk.

The Field of Faith

Carl smiles despite the torrents of rain at Soldier Field.

Billed as the Archdiocese's highlight of the Jubilee Year, the Field of Faith on June 24, 2000 was held in an open air cathedral created in Chicago's Soldier Field.

For a crowd of thirty thousand, the event included two hours of musical presentations, and a Mass led by Francis Cardinal George. Hundreds of parish and community banners were proudly carried into the stadium by the faithful in an Olympian-style parade. Others walked from Chicago's Little Village and Pilsen neighborhoods to worship God in the grand setting.

A sixty-piece orchestra accompanied a specially-created jubilee choir, and original hymns were composed and sung gloriously by mostly parish-based musical groups.

For many worshipers, the first sight as they approached Soldier Field via Lake Shore Drive was Our Lady of the New Millennium standing in quiet dignity. She had been placed there with great deliberation to provide a welcome to the festive event.

However, worshipers were challenged by the heavy downpour that characterized the entire event. Cardinal George called it "the longest sprinkling rite ever recorded in liturgical history."

The rain never gave up, but neither did the people who gathered for the event of the Millennium. People continued singing and praying, kneeling and standing as if the torrent were merely a drizzle.

As Carmelo and Anna Schifano, accompanied by Carl and Francine Demma, approached Soldier Field, Carl told Schifano to stop the car and let him out at the foot of the statue so he could pass out holy cards. Carmelo says, "He passed out tons of cards. He was in heaven!"

Carl's friend, Peter Coppa, recalls, "During the service I said to Carl, 'You told me before the statue was even built that one day the statue would be at Soldier Field, and here it is, like you said.' Carl said to me, 'I told you it might take a miracle, but that it was going to happen. Peter, I have fulfilled my dream.'"

Eventually Carl joined his friends, all sitting with umbrellas in the incessant rain. Carmen reports, "I think Carl had walking pneumonia. I told him we had to get out of there, but he insisted on staying because he wanted to receive communion from Cardinal George."

Schifano says, "We were sitting in the back, but Carl stood up and said, 'Follow me.' We followed him right up to the front. His coughing was getting worse, and he promised that he would leave right after we received communion.

"As we were leaving, Carl said to me, 'I finally did it! I did what I had to do.'"

Farewell

After leaving Soldier Field, Demma asked Schifano to drive him to the north side of Chicago to St. Stanislaus Kostka Church to see the statue of The Divine Mercy that had just arrived. Carl had agreed to serve as custodian for the statue when it went on tour.

They returned to the Demma's house, and Carl seemed to be on top of the world. He confided to Schifano, "Now that the statue is completed, I am finally relaxed. I am finally finding a little contentment.

"I've had great joy in my life, and I'm so grateful to have known my daughters and the joy they brought to me and my wife. I don't question God. People don't understand that things don't always turn out the way we want them to, but the way God wants them to.

"This has been a great day."

After ordering Chinese, Carl gave Carmelo a big hug and went to bed.

The next morning, he wakened Fran to go to St. Jerome's Church to hear a priest from Medjugorje. Later, after a bite to eat, Fran went to a bridal shower, and Carl went to St. Stanislaus Kostka to pray before the Blessed Divine Mercy statue. On the way home, he stopped for ice cream.

When he didn't return home, Francine became worried. Finally, she glanced out the front door and saw their car in the driveway. She ran out and found Carl still behind the wheel – the victim of a heart attack.

Father Fragomeni arranged for The Shrine of Pompeii's statue of Padre Pio to be transported to Carl's wake, and it stood right next to the coffin. There was a great demand for the holy cards featuring Our Lady of the New Millennium. Father Fragomeni said, "Everyone knew who Carl Demma was. I felt good passing out the cards."

Cardinal George issued a statement saying, "*The death of Mr. Carl Demma is a great loss for me and for all those who loved him and benefited from his love of the Virgin Mary. He was known to Catholics in the Archdiocese of Chicago for his commissioning of the beautiful sculpture of Our Lady of the New Millennium.*

Mr. Demma had tremendous love for Mary, the Mother of God, and great trust in Our Lord. The people of the Archdiocese of Chicago are indebted to him and to his family, and we commend him to the mercy of God, that he might soon be with the Lord, his Blessed Mother, and the angels and saints to enjoy the vision of God in eternity.

The funeral Mass for Carl Demma was held at Holy Name Cathedral. As Francine arrived at the cathedral, she beheld the Knights of Columbus guard of honor in their blue regalia on the steps of the cathedral.

Father Tony Markus presided at the funeral Mass, and Cardinal George rearranged his schedule in order to be co-celebrant. At Francine's request, Father Richard Fragomeni presented the homily.

Father Fragomeni spoke of the many moments in Jesus' life when Mary was present. In the temple, at the wedding in Cana, when Christ was dying on the cross, on Pentecost Thursday, Mary was right there.

"Last Saturday, at the millennium celebration at Soldier Field," Mary was also right there," he said. "She has certainly been there in the life of Carl Demma. No doubt, when Carl was called by God, Mary was right there to welcome him. And as we continue our journey, Millennium Mary will always be there to remind us that we have a mother and to share the affection of our brothers and sisters in Christ."

He spoke of Carl Demma as "someone who weathered all kinds of storms and still had hope and faith. When you were with him, you always had a sense of comfort, knowing no matter how bad things got, he still had a sense of hope. His statue was big, and he was a big man with a solidness and a real sense of beauty."

Photo provided by James Krischokas, Chicago, IL.

Perhaps the most fitting eulogy was the following, written by a sixth grader, Michelle Bruno, when her class was asked to write about a saint for All Saints Day:

Dear Carl,

You were always there for me, and you always made me happy when I was down. I loved hearing your stories about why you made the Millennium statue of Mary and what encouraged you to continue to live your dream.

You are a holy man, and you will always be that to me. You believed in God and His Kingdom. Everyone loved you, and we will keep you in our hearts.

You made me feel like you were my dad. When you died, I felt like I couldn't have anyone like you again in my life. I am very happy to have your wife, Fran, in my life.

When I listened to the Cardinal at your funeral and what he said about taking walks with God every day, but one day God asked you to come into His Kingdom and you followed. Now you are home.

I know that you did so many great things in your life, but you never wanted to brag about them. You were a quiet man who had such a devotion to Mary, the Mother of God. You helped so many people come back to the faith and pray to Mary for their own special needs. We needed someone like that in our lives.

I consider you to be a saint because you were such a good person. You lived a holy life of praying and going to church. I will always remember you, now and forever.

Love, Michelle

Leaving Holy Name Cathedral, the stream of cars escorting Carl Demma on his last journey was indicative of a man who had touched so many lives. The Chicago police responded by closing off every side street going south on Lake Shore Drive so the cavalcade could proceed uninterrupted.

When Carl and those who loved him arrived at Holy Sepulchre Cemetery, Our Lady of the New Millennium was waiting there.

▲ The sun pierces the heart of Our Lady – St. Michael's Parish, Orland Park, IL

Top – Candles, flowers, and notes are offered in abundance everywhere Our Lady appears.
Bottom Left – A Sweet 16 celebration is one of the many occasions to take a picture with Our Lady of the New Millennium.
Bottom Right – Navy Pier, Chicago, Illinois

Top – Our Lady towers over a nearby barn on Chicago's south side.
Bottom – Over 300 students of Maria High School in Chicago, Illinois gather to welcome Our Lady.

Assembling Our Lady outside
Charles Parks' studio in
Wilmington, Delaware

The Demmas donated three more statues to the people of Chicago.

- A life-sized statue of Padre Pio in honor of their daughters, Carla and Judy, to the Shrine of Pompeii.
- Our Lady of Guadalupe to St. Pius Church.
- Mother Teresa holding a baby in her hands to the Convent of the Missionaries of Charity.

With the Sears Tower beside her, Our Lady stands at the John Paul II Newman Center at the University of Illinois – Chicago.

Top – The winter home of Our Lady of the New Millennium – Sacred Heart Parish, Palos Hills, Illinois.
Left – The moon gently illuminates Our Lady's face at St. Bruno's in Chicago, IL.

In Remembrance of

Our Lady of the

New Millennium

St. John Brebeuf Church

September 17-27, 1999

Hail Mary Full of Grace
The Lord is With Thee ....

Carl - Thank you for bringing Mary into the new Millenium with such beauty, grace, and dignity.

The Sable Family
Wendy, Jim, Matthew, and Baby #2

A beautiful way to refocus our priorities going into a new age.
Thank you
Caroline

Dear Mr. Demma,
It is so nice to see something so positive and holy - then all the bad things going on. Thank you.
Joyce (Chica

Mr. Demma,
Thanks for a once in a life time celebration
Maria

Dear Mr Demma
You have given so much Hope and Faith with this Wonderful Statue. I also believe we all will see her very soon!
Mrs Aneta Ostrege

Thank you for putting such Beauty & grace into a Masterpiece that speaks in words to match its sight! a work of art!
Lori Matt

A beautiful work of art in a time when mankind really needs to get back on track to what is important. Thank you! Your gift is a wonderful reminder to us all as to what is important now and in the coming millenium.

9-21-99
Divinely inspired; Beautiful artistry! Thank you Carl - Thank you Charles
H. Nemish

A portrait of Our Lady of the New Millennium
in pencil by MaryAnn H. Skutta. Copyright 2003.

Our Lady's Travels Begin

As Our Lady of the New Millennium fulfilled the dreams of Carl Demma, traveling to the faithful and the seeking throughout Chicagoland, each visit was fresh and new for the people who came to see her.

She usually arrived very early in the morning before rush hour traffic made transportation difficult. Frequently, many people rose before dawn to be on hand to greet her and welcome her with prayers and song.

Before their eyes, the statue lying quietly on the Marian blue trailer begins to rise up – slowly, slowly, slowly – until she towers above the people and many of the buildings nearby. The experience of watching the statue of the Blessed Mother rise up to her towering height immediately draws awe and exclamations,

Flowers, gifts and messages were brought by the dozens.

bringing tears to many eyes.

Initially people think it's a colossal statue, and that's it. But when they're in her presence, it's a whole different feeling.

After taking in the scale and grace of the work, spectators usually move in for a closer inspection. Trying to figure out how the statue is supported, they peek inside the spot-welded strips of stainless steel that drape the work and give it a bright and fluid appearance. Often they walk around it, sometimes circling two or three times. Then they reach out and touch her. Everybody seems to want to touch the statue, so the drivers position the statue so people can easily approach it.

Soon more and more people arrive. They come in the sunshine and in the rain. They come during the day and throughout the night. A hushed reverence sets the tone as hundreds of people settle in lawn chairs, many remaining for hours to pray or just to gaze at her.

Many arrive with hearts on sleeves, hoping for instant answers to desperate prayers. Families come with children. Some come looking for miracles, often hobbling behind walkers or seated in wheelchairs. Some, old themselves, bring their parents. Men and women come from every walk of life and many ethnic traditions.

Some just come to feel God's love in the company of others who show their faith.

Many are visitors from out of town or from another country who have been brought to her by their family members. Frequently, visitors follow the statue from town to town.

Every parish has a story or two to tell, but mostly the story is the same – it draws the community together.

The statue encourages members of the diverse communities that make up a parish to share religious and cultural appreciation. Many who come to see her are of other faiths, but they, too, are awed by her beauty and power. Drawn like a magnet, they come on their own personal pilgrimages in a steady stream of faith.

One nun said, "I've visited several different settings with different classes of people in different neighborhoods, and yet there is a common denominator. There is a sort of spirit and response of faith and love of the people in each of them. "It's like little pilgrimages into people's own neighborhoods. They can't go to Lourdes, France, but they can go to a parking lot next to a church or convent."

They bring roses, potted plants, and candles. They bring pictures of loved ones, sick or lost. Standing in her shadow, ordinary people speak of extraordinary struggles, of joy, of salvation, and of the transforming power of prayer.

Since visitors want to know more about the statue and about Carl Demma, many of the churches and other sites she visited prepared and distributed literature telling the story of the statue and that of the man whose dream she embodies.

There is seldom a moment when someone isn't with Mary, singing, praying, quietly watching, weeping. Men cry, women sob. Dozens of rosaries of every color pass through the fingers of those praying before the thirty-three-foot statue.

Many of the visitors leave written prayers, either publicly in a book or privately in a small box. Prayer request boxes are often filled quickly, and must be emptied several times a day. Some of the prayers are for family members, others for an end to racial injustice and for peace in the world.

Many slip their written prayers into the slits in her garments.

People at each site seize the opportunity of the statue's visit to celebrate and worship in their own way, whether by Masses, daily reciting of the Rosary, or other special ways.

Security is never a problem. There have been no attempts to vandalize or steal the statue.

Carl Demma's dream continues to draw amazement and wonder from the many who behold her, whether for the first time or upon her eagerly anticipated return visits. Virtually everywhere she appears, people beg to have her return.

At each appearance of the statue, there is something new, something amazing, something spiritually awakening for those who come to see her.

In Their Words

The following chapters share stories about lives she has touched during some of her visits.

From a priest: "People are coming, not only from the neighborhood, but all over the south and north suburbs. The intention of the statue is to bring Catholics and Christians back to the faith. I think it's happening."

A deacon at a Skokie church: "Each of our groups has a slightly different tradition, but sharing this, we become a more united family of faith. As diverse as we are, this is an icon for all groups."

One observer noted, "I first saw her in a neighborhood on the south side of the city where the houses were mostly bungalows and not very large. The statue loomed over these small homes. Because of the contrast in size, it was almost frightening."

Joe S. wrote, "I was personally touched during her visit to Transfiguration Parish in Wauconda. My life had undergone a series of challenges that made me question my faith, the pure essence of my existence. My prayer life had become routine, and I felt my obligation to God and Our Lord Jesus Christ was fulfilled through attendance at Sunday Mass.

"Our pastor's verbal description of the statue to be displayed in the church parking lot was impressive, but I cannot begin to state how inadequate his words seemed when I saw this beautiful statue honoring Our Blessed Mother.

"As I knelt in prayer, I was both awed and truly humbled as I realized how weak my faith had become. The words spoken by Mary at the wedding at Cana finally took hold... 'do whatever He tells you.' I realized how prideful I had become and how insignificant I truly was (still am).

"Our Lady of the New Millennium inspired me in her grandness, humbled me with her size, and comforted me with her beauty.

At Festa Italiana on Milwaukee's lakefront, Kathleen S., who suffered from a heart condition, said, "I don't care what religion you are, it gives you the feeling that God is so close."

Michael Rosenberg, a Jewish lawyer who was a friend of Carl's, was attending a Catholic lawyers' dinner in Chicago. Cardinal George was at this same dinner, and since Michael had met him at Carl's funeral, they began to discuss Carl. Michael says, "We agreed that Carl was quite a guy. He realized that dreams stay alive, and in the end, look what his dream has done for other people. That is a miracle!"

At St. Constance Parish in Chicago, a man wrote, "I love the fold of her hands, not quite clasped in prayer, but headed in that direction. I love the expression on her face, not quite smiling, but looking like she knows some wonderful secret involving us that it isn't yet time to reveal. I love her eyes, big, round, and open wide. To borrow a line from 'Good Vibrations', my all-time favorite Beach Boys song, 'I loved the way the sunlight played upon her hair'.

"But what really caught and held my attention were the delicate ribbons of stainless steel that make up her garment and cloak. There is a delicate openness to the figure that allows me to see right through it ~ the trees, the sky. Indeed, on one of my visits, I saw three sparrows in flight. Even as they disappeared behind the statue, I could still see them fluttering for an instant through the fine latticework of steel before they came back into full view."

In Lansing, Illinois, twin boys, Charlie and Sammy, both have cerebral palsy. Their mother first took them to see Our Lady of the New Millennium when they were three years old. They have gone to several different parishes to see her, and both, especially Charlie, are infatuated with her. He looks at the statue's web site and takes the photos his mother took of the statue to school for Show and Tell. He remembers the day his mother let him get up close so he could touch her toes.

At St. Lambert, a man said he was most affected by the rainbow of colors that sunlight creates on the stainless steel surface of the statue.

A woman, whose visit left her brushing away tears, said she had seen Our Lady of the New Millennium three times. Seeing the statue helped her communicate with Mary.

A woman in Evergreen Park was apprehensive because doctors had been skeptical about the health of her unborn triplet granddaughters. She came to the statue to give thanks for the recent birth of three healthy girls.

Theresa B. of Chicago came to pray for the success of her husband, Frank, who recently underwent surgery. "I just want him to get better, and this is the best thing I know to do," she said.

Loren B. said, "When the statue came to San Rocco Oratory, I stood before her and felt as if I was standing before Jesus himself! Something just came over me that made me feel so humble. I was in awe of her. I still feel like breaking out in goose pimples whenever I tell about the experience. It was truly awesome."

When Barbara C. took her four-year-old grandson, Sam, to

visit the statue at St. Zachary Parish in Des Plaines, he kept looking at her face. All the way back to their seats, his head was turned toward her. Finally, he asked, "Nanny, what does she want?" Barbara explained that she wanted them to love her Son Jesus and to pray for peace in the world. With his innocent eyes focused on Our Lady, Sam said, "Oh, we can do that!"

Daniela Occelli and her son visit with Francine and Our Lady.

Daniela Occelli, who as a seventeen-year-old came to stay with the Demmas for a year as an Italian exchange student, recalls, "The very first night, Carl talked to me about the difference between Italy and America, how in America people feel they have to have a big car, a big house, lots of money.

"And on the first night, he told me about the statue and showed me the three-foot mold he had. I kept looking at it and thinking, 'You're going to build a thirty-three-foot statue? I couldn't believe it!

"After I knew the Demmas better, I understood more. Knowing them changed my life. I was a Catholic and went to church, but I didn't really question my faith or ask myself questions.

"When I saw their faith, even with the loss of two daughters, it was unreal to me – the openness they had, and the way they related to people.

"Carl was able to talk to anybody, anywhere. He helped me understand what faith could be.

"This was so different from Italy where you sit at Mass and then go home, and that's it. Carl believed so much. He wanted the statue to bring back people's faith.

"Later, when I finally saw the statue, I just looked at him. It was the fulfillment of a lifetime for him. I was so glad I was able to see him one more time after the statue was built, and I told him, 'Carl, I'm so happy. You did it!'

"I was so happy God was able to see his faith!"

St. Patrick's Church

Because one of the parishioners at St. Patrick's Church in St. Charles, Illinois, had aided Carl Demma with the arrangements in St. Louis, St. Patrick's was one of the early churches the statue visited.

Msgr. Joseph B. Linster recalled, "I had a meeting with the personnel director of the diocese, and he said, 'By the way, someone is going to contact you about a big statue. You may think he is a kook – but he isn't. He's an honest, upright gentleman, very much on the up and up. Listen to him."

Msgr. Linster understood far better when he had the opportunity to meet and talk to Carl and Francine Demma. Carl mentioned the number of people who came to see the statue and to spend time in prayer. "The reason they come" he said, "is that people are hungry..." Although he didn't elaborate, Msgr. Linster knew that Demma hoped and prayed that Our Lady of the New Millennium would ease the hunger within the spirits of those who visited her. He prayed that, through her, people would be drawn closer to the Lord and listen more closely to the sound of His voice. Linster said, "When Mary leads us to the feet of Jesus, her ultimate purpose has been achieved, for it is at His feet that our hunger will be satisfied."

Subsequently Frank Smoczynski of Linster's parish contacted him to help with arrangements for the statue's visit. This was the first time the statue would go to a site where Adoration of the Blessed Sacrament was encouraged and promoted the belief that true devotion to Mary should ultimately lead to her Son. If it doesn't, the fullness that Marian devotions have to offer is not achieved.

Carl and Francine with Frank Smoczynski.

Our Lady of the New Millennium arrived on a chilly, misty April day. "When I first saw her," Linster said, "I thought, "My goodness. Fools do rush in."

"Then I stood there as she rose. Wow! A crowd had gathered, and flowers were spread around the base of the truck. It was just gorgeous."

The statue was placed between the church rectory and the school, across the street from a city park. The City of St. Charles cooperated by turning off all nearby lighting at night and installing a spotlight on a telephone pole to burn throughout the night. Church personnel set up chairs in the park. "It became like a little shrine. It was an ideal location," said Linster.

Others brought CD players to share church music before the statue.

Visitors were encouraged to proceed from the statue into the church where the Adoration was held every day, and the sacrament was exposed so people could walk in and see it.

Senior residents and others arrived by the busload. Linster's own mother came frequently to sit in the park and say her Rosary.

One day, three sisters from Mother Teresa's order, the Missionaries of Charity, came. They remarked how inspiring the statue was for them, and one commented, "My heart is full of love for her."

Bishop Doran of Rockford came to celebrate Mass for the Feast of the Assumption. "It was the perfect setting," said Linster.

Linster himself, dressed informally, often sat in the midst of the gathered crowd and listened to families praying the Rosary with their children. He recalls a young family who sat on a large blanket they had brought. Each took a rosary from their pocket and began praying together. Each took a turn leading the Rosary and praying from a meditation book as the mysteries were announced. Finally, Msgr. Linster asked if they did this often. "Every day," they said.

A guest book was filled with thousands of names, including those of visitors from Germany, France, Sweden, and Spain. Perfect Plastic Printing provided holy cards with a picture of the statue on one side and the Memorare on the back. This card has continued to be available throughout the statue's travels.

At one point, an ambulance drove up to St. Patrick's with lights flashing. The driver opened the door, and onlookers saw a woman in a hospital gown with an IV in her arm. She appeared very relaxed and peaceful, just looking at the statue and saying her prayers before Our Lady of the New Millennium.

A man from Rockford wrote, "My daughter brought us to see the Lady of the New Millennium. Absolutely incredible! An invisible spiritual cloud hovers over your city. Its impact cannot be humanly measured."

When his family drove up to the church, four-year-old David, without any coaching, ran across the street, knelt down, put his hands together, and began praying.

A nine-year-old girl with leukemia came every day with her mother. She wanted to see "the Giant Lady."

A mariachi band came to serenade at five in the morning.

Many staff and volunteers led prayers, led songs, made sure

Carl hands out Memorare cards.

handouts were printed, notified the media and other parishes around the area, and answered questions: What time are the devotions? How do I get to St. Patrick's? How long will she be here? Where will she be going after she leaves St. Patrick's?

Although there was a great opportunity for frayed nerves and short tempers, none were seen. Thousands of people came together with nothing more on their minds than to see the statue and spend time in prayer.

The twenty-five thousand plastic Memorare cards printed for the three week visit were gone by the second week. More had to be printed. Not once were these cards seen thrown on the ground or in the trash container. They will be in peoples' homes, prayer books, purses, and pockets for years to come.

Thousands of dollars were collected for the poor. The Demmas wanted absolutely nothing to do with that money, nor would they take any donation from the parish for allowing use of the statue. It was their gift to the parish.

Arlene Patton, a member of the church, said, "This is bringing us to Jesus through her. We have Eucharistic devotions, and the church has been full. We're in awe of how many people are here for the Rosary, for the devotions, and the Adoration. I've been running out of handouts. I love it!"

During the statue's second visit a year later, St. Patrick's hosted an International Living Rosary in the park across the street. Many foreign languages were used in leading the Rosary.

There was also an outdoor Eucharistic Healing Service. The following day, a children's Living Rosary was prayed in the park.

In his weekly pastor's letter, Fr. Linster said, "I must admit that I didn't realize all the ramifications of this event. However, the privilege of having Our Lady of the New Millennium with us, the many prayers and devotions she inspires by being here, and the many graces and blessings that are ours by her presence will far outweigh anything that had to be done to make it possible for her to be with us. To Jesus through Mary!"

The Visions of Oscar Mendez

When Oscar Mendez went to pick up his children up at school one day in 1999, he had no idea it was a day that would change his life.

As he drove along he beheld, to his amazement and with no warning, an incredible sight – an indescribably beautiful thirty-three-foot tall shimmering steel Madonna.

"I came back the next day," he recalls, "and took some photographs. I returned every day that week. On the last day of the statue's visit, I met Carl Demma and gave him a few photographs I had taken.

"He told me he liked my pictures. He especially liked the photo I had taken with the moon behind her and tears in her eyes."

Carl asked Oscar to meet him at the next parish to which the statue was being transported. He wanted Oscar to take more photographs. Mendez continued traveling with the statue and recording her visits on film.

"My initial idea," he said, "was to sell the pictures I took. I felt I could make a lot of money." He asked for Carl Demma's approval, and Carl answered that it was all right with him if the parishes approved, but he didn't want to be involved in any way.

"But I didn't feel good about it," said Oscar. "My objective was changing. I didn't know exactly why I was following her as she moved from parish to parish, but I just kept taking the pictures.

"There were people who wanted to take professional pictures with very good equipment. I didn't have professional equipment or a car, but Carl chose me. He'd pick me up at my house and drive me to the church or give me a ride back home.

"At the end of the year, my son, Oscar, was constructing web pages. I asked him if he would make up a web page for me. I bought the rights to a web site (now www.ourladyofthemillennium.com) and asked the Demmas for their approval. They said it was all right with them.

"The web site was up and running at the beginning of 2000. I put something up on the web site from each parish I visited." Thousands of people visit the web site from all over the country and beyond.

The last time Oscar saw Carl Demma, Carl was at Maryville Academy giving out holy cards to a group of children.

The gentle face of Our Lady as captured by Oscar Mendez.

When Carl Demma passed away, Mendez wasn't sure he had the heart to continue with his work. "I didn't know if the statue would continue to travel," he said, "but Mrs. Demma shared my vision. She urged me to continue the work.

"My life was changing. In my younger years, I was very active in the Church, but now I was not living a spiritual life. I saw all of these people going to different parishes and the faith they had in the Mother of God. I saw how Mr. and Mrs. Demma had given everything for this vision. I realized that I had a vision, too, and that it was growing. I didn't need to be rich or famous. I could use my talents."

Oscar Mendez had learned the art of photography many years before when he had an accident at work and had to look for a less physical profession. He took up photography and worked on a freelance basis.

"Mainly, I did news photography and was active in politics," he said. He was assigned to cover the Pope's 1979 visit to Chicago and became known for the commemorative booklet and local newspaper articles he produced.

Mendez visited virtually every parish at which Our Lady of the New Millennium appeared, generally traveling by bus, as he didn't own a car. "I could see the results of Our Lady's visits, spiritually, economically, materially," he said. "More people would come to that parish, groups would organize within the church, and more people volunteered their services and participated in different ways."

At parish after parish, people would talk to Oscar about the amazing things they had experienced. "I've seen people dying who asked to die in peace or to be cured. At one parish, I saw a guy coming along with a bottle of liquor, talking to himself. He looked up at the statue and dropped his bottle. The wind picked it up and carried it out into the street; although it didn't seem to me there was any wind. The man got so scared, he started crying. He knelt down and asked for pardon, saying he was going to give up the alcohol."

Mendez's activities inspired him to become increasingly involved in church affairs, especially with the Queen of the Americas Guild. He said, "There is a faith in all of us, but sometimes it is a sleeping faith. Sometimes we need something to wake it up.

"Everybody can do something. I give my talent and my time."

A Special Place

Sacred Heart Parish in Palos Hills, Illinois, has had a very special relationship with Our Lady of the New Millennium. It was one of the first places the statue visited in its travels.

Carl Demma had talked to Fr. Robert McGinnity a great deal about the statue during its construction, but when Fr. McGinnity saw pictures of the many jagged edges of steel, he found it difficult to picture how they would all be matched up.

However, he told Carl that Sacred Heart would be happy to host the statue. "Although," he said, "I didn't know what we'd do with it!"

Initial plans were simple. There would be Marian devotions every evening for whoever wished to come. Since "Our Lady of the New Millennium" was a new title, it was decided to celebrate Marian devotions while incorporating some of the other beautiful titles of Mary. Never did anyone imagine how greatly the Spirit would take over and multiply these efforts.

Performers at Sacred Heart in traditional Polish dress.

The plan was to say the first decade of the Rosary in English and then invite people to join in in their own language. Each night it would be said in a different language, and often there would be a hymn in the language of the night.

After weeks of recruiting individuals to lead the Rosary in various languages, the staff was a little nervous because, for some languages, there were only one or two people available to lead the prayers. However, when the evening came to recognize the Marian traditions in those countries, three or five or ten new members joined the volunteers in saying the prayers.

Fr. McGinnity said, "We thought we were generous when we planned for five hundred participants the first evening, but our programs ran out quickly. We thought we were optimistic when we increased the count to one thousand – but God sent twelve hundred faithful instead.

Marine Corps color guard.

"When the skies threatened to break forth in deluges of rain, we were worried that we would not be able to fit those twelve hundred into the church. What a miracle it was to watch the rains fall before and after the evening devotions, but never at the time of the devotions themselves.

"For our final night's celebration honoring Mary as the patroness of the United States, we really thought we were being accommodating when we printed two thousand programs. God sent almost three thousand souls to join the praise chorus!

"Then, when we thought for sure we would fall short of feeding those multitudes at our 'Taste of Sweets,' we were amazed to learn that we had quite a lot of leftovers."

During the statue's two-week visit, devotions ranged from honors to Our Lady of the Dawn (Lithuania) and Our Lady of Ettal (Germany) to Mae Phra (India) and Zaragoza (Spain).

The second year, observances included half an hour of sharing the cultural heritage of the featured country. Lithuanians brought their flag, and Poles brought two flags. French people brought a miniature Eiffel Tower, and an opera singer performed on Italian night.

Irish dancers danced, and Scotsmen played the bagpipes.

When a Korean girl in the parish was asked to say the Rosary in Korean, she arrived with a busload of women in Korean costume.

The final night, featuring Our Lady of the Immaculate Conception (the United States), included a man in uniform just back from Iraq and Afghanistan and a policeman who had been called to form a police department in Baghdad. There was a Marine Corps color guard, as well as representatives of the U.S. Navy and Air Force.

The statue was always lighted all night, and a steady stream of people came, night and day. There were two hospitals nearby, and after midnight a number of nurses would come and spend considerable time. In the middle of the night, about fifty Hispanic people who worked at a mail order house close by came for forty-five minutes.

One morning, Fr. McGinnity saw a semi belonging to a landscaping company drive up. The driver hopped out of the truck, went up and prayed, and got back into the truck and drove off.

The beauty of the services inspired many to write to the church afterward.

From Oak Forest: "I felt as though she was not only there

Our Lady's prayerful gaze greets the crowd at Sacred Heart parish.

spiritually, but alive, touching all who were present. The service was the most beautiful I have ever been a part of, and it will remain with me forever."

From Milwaukee: "Most impressive was the reverent peaceful spirit of all who came to spend precious time with her. The parishioners of Sacred Heart who reached out to me with a warm welcome reminded me of the kindly, humble villages of Medjugorje when I visited there. The Christ-like spirit of hospitality permeated the area."

From Chicago Ridge: "I was so pleased to see your sense of fairness in including every group in your parish. Clearly, the Lord has blessed you with uncommon depth that allows you to embrace all regardless of color or ethnicity."

From Tiburon, California: "I was recently in Chicago to attend my father-in-law's funeral. As we all know, funerals are not easy on anyone, so the reason I'm writing is to thank you and your family. Thank you for having the beautiful statue of the Virgin Mary which was set up at her resting place, the Sacred Heart Church. The presence of Our Lady of the New Millennium comforted me and my family during a difficult time in our lives. We placed flowers at her feet after the funeral. Her motherly figure looking down on us made us feel so much better. What a great gift you and your family have given to the people of Chicago."

From Palos Heights: "We still talk about the beautiful two weeks with Our Lady of the New Millennium. It was so wonderful how you brought the parish together with Our Lady. We still say that was the most beautiful two weeks of our lives."

During the second year of the statue's travels, Carl said to Fr. McGinnity, "I have a surprise for you," and told him that Our Lady of the New Millennium could come to spend the winter on Sacred Heart's spacious grounds. The statue has spent every winter there since, and people have continued to come to visit her and pray during the day and through the night.

The Resurrection Project

Since 1990, a group of churches in southwest Chicago's Pilsen area have been joined in The Resurrection Project. Blooming in the heart of Chicago's vibrant Mexican community, the faith-based Resurrection Project challenges people to act on their faith and values to create healthy communities.

Beginning with six member parishes committing $5,000 in seed capital, the initial $30,000 has grown to over $120 million in community investment. With twelve churches now in the project, it has taken the form of commercial development, increased affordable housing units, small business support, and loan assistance for first-time homebuyers.

When Pilsen residents first learned Our Lady of the New Millennium was appearing in one of her early visits at a nearby parish, Fr. Chuck Niehaus of St. Procopius contacted Francine Demma with a request that Our Lady be brought to the Pilsen area.

In the neighborhoods served by The Resurrection Project, street Masses are a cherished tradition, and driving through the area, one often runs into streets closed for Mass. On Sunday, people go to church. Monday through Saturday, the church goes to them.

As part of the annual End of Summer celebration, a street Mass is held on the zocalo (plaza) in front of The Resurrection Project's offices. Traditionally, the Cardinal has attended, as have other high church officials. Hundreds of people come to this service.

In 2003 and 2004, Our Lady of the New Millennium was the

The Pilsen Resurrection Project draws visitors from near and far.

most honored guest at the End of Summer celebration. Each night of the week, one church in The Resurrection Project held the bilingual Mass. The same church sponsored an overnight vigil by the people of its parish.

Readings during the Mass concentrated on social issues such as education, health, and social justice, with time for personal testimonies.

An observer said, "Nice weather, rainy weather, sometimes people were singing, sometimes saying the Rosary, but she was never alone."

Three tables were set out to receive candles, and these were always filled to capacity. Each day great quantities of flowers were placed at her feet.

Alvaro Obregon, a facilitator of The Resurrection Project, said, "We see people in wheelchairs and many older people often praying for a miracle or praying for strength to get through their illnesses."

One twelve year-old girl went to every Mass.

One evening, members of a musical group that had finished its regular gig around three in the morning came to the plaza with their instruments and led the people there in songs of praise.

On the day Our Lady was to leave the zocalo early in the morning, people who wanted to honor the Blessed Virgin gathered in the plaza at 5 a.m., some taking the day off from work. There was no opportunity to hold a Mass before the truck and driver arrived, but over two hundred people came to celebrate Las Mananitas, a traditional serenade performed at dawn on an individual's birthday. They continued singing until almost 9 a.m. when the truck arrived.

The people who live in the area of The Resurrection Project have taken Our Lady of the New Millennium as their own. When it became known that she would not be available for the End of Summer Mass in 2005, Obregon asked people on the streets if they would still want her to come a month later. He received replies like "Of course we want her. What kind of a question is that?" Others had tears in their eyes at the thought that she might not come.

On August 19, 2003, seven-year-old Ana Mateo, with her family, visited Our Lady of the New Millennium. Ana asked if the Virgin Mary was in heaven, and her mother said yes. Ana asked if there were angels in heaven, and her mother told her they were in heaven and everywhere.

Ana asked, "How do I become an angel?" Her mother said, "Some day you'll become an angel."

That hot night, after Ana returned home, a bullet from the gun of a gang member who was chasing a rival gang member traveled a block and a half and struck Ana in the head.

Now each year, Ana's mother comes to see Our Lady of the New Millennium bearing flowers and a banner with a picture of Ana that says, "In loving memory -- we'll always remember you."

A Big Problem at St. Christopher

At St. Christopher Parish in Midlothian, Illinois, Our Lady of the New Millennium's coming was foretold in bulletin and newspaper, by telephone and e-mail. Her arrival was announced with blue ribbon tied to trees and light posts.

A parishioner said, "We were quickly sprinkled, then baptized, with torrents of rain that very first day. We were washed clean, and the Spirit blew in our midst. We were children gazing up at our loving Mother. She returned our gaze and reflected our own desires for the goodness and love of God."

A sister from Nigeria led the evening Rosary and witnessed that she had received personal assistance from Mary in the payment of a large bill.

A family along with their friends prayed frequently and fervently for the recovery of a family member with cancer. One evening, tears of joy were shared when the news was received that his tumor had shrunk and surgery would not be required.

One woman told of the reaction of her neighbor to her description of the statue and the visitation. His emotional response surprised and touched her. The young man had been out of work for a long time and feeling hopeless, but something stirred within him when he heard of the presence of Our Lady of the New Millennium at St. Christopher, and finally he went to see her. The very next day, his young sister ran to tell the woman that Jose had been given a job. She proudly pointed to the truck he would be driving.

The pictures of two servicemen who had been brutally murdered in Iraq were placed at the feet of the statue and remained through the wind and the rain for nineteen days. A woman commented, "She seemed to be letting us know that she had cared for them and would care for us as well."

A young woman who came to visit every day said, "I'm not Catholic, but I know that she's my mother."

But St. Christopher was a parish that was suffering deeply and was in great trouble. A trusted member of the parish who carried the main responsibility for the management of its finances had been found to be dishonest. In addition to mismanaging the finances, he had also been stealing a significant amount of money. The parish was deeply in debt and didn't see how it could work its way out.

The new pastor assigned to St. Christopher, Fr. Mark Walter, prayed with Our Lady alone every morning, and other members of the parish were also praying fervently.

The Archdiocese offered support to the parish, somewhat easing the burden, but the debt was still overwhelming. Then a parishioner approached Fr. Mark, saying that, if the Archdiocese would match it, he would contribute a substantial amount.

This left the parish still in debt, but one that was manageable. By holding fundraisers and a pledge drive, St. Christopher parish was debt free just one year after Our Lady of the New Millennium visited.

During Her Travels...

In Lemont, Illinois, there was a joint effort by all of the parishes and Catholic institutions in the village. During the week of her stay, each parish, as well as other facilities, had an afternoon or evening in which they were in charge of the events. The Village of Lemont issued a proclamation welcoming the statue.

Roman Catholic representatives of all of Lemont's Scout troops renewed their pledges to God and country at Our Lady of the New Millennium on the rolling incline at Mt. Assisi Academy. Worshipers said birds flying overhead under billowing white clouds momentarily broke their innate patterns, forming a living crown shadowing the statue's head.

At St. Eugene Parish, when Our Lady of the New Millennium visited, firemen and policemen held their own special service.

Our Lady of the New Millennium was present at Knanaya Catholic Center for a Mass and a twenty-four-hour vigil. The center is located across the street from an abortion clinic.

After Mass, the faithful processed to the parking lot where they surrounded the statue, which was facing the abortion clinic. When devotions concluded after two hours, many of the faithful remained to pray, while others joined the vigil.

Throughout the night, the faithful took turns leading prayer.

Counselors outside the abortion clinic offered alternatives to abortion-bound moms. It was reported that three women who planned to abort their babies changed their minds that day.

One person commented, "Our Lady of the New Millennium

brought a presence of holiness to the entire neighborhood. Having the statue there as a witness for the unborn was like a dream come true."

In Waukegan, neighbors who had not spoken hugged and prayed together. An elderly man came most mornings to play religious songs on his harmonica. He is Unitarian and married to a Jewish woman.

One hundred and two year-old Paz Najano was drawn to the statue twice.

One hundred and two year-old Paz Najano came not once, but twice to see Our Lady. Paz has one child, nine grandchildren, twenty-eight great-grandchildren and eighteen great-great-grandchildren.

Outdoor celebrations offered familiar religious language to Hispanic residents of one Chicago neighborhood, many of whom were new arrivals. They also helped to reach those who don't usually attend church. One sister commented that the atmosphere in the neighborhood improves when a community gets to know each other, see each other, and get together. Events such as an outdoor Mass can make those kinds of encounters happen.

A group playing religious songs alternated verses in English and Spanish, but it was not hard to tell which was preferred by the crowd. The voices singing the verses in Spanish were louder, and so were the ones answering prayers spoken in Spanish.

At a Mass dedicated to young people, a group of teens presented a basketball. Another boy watched the Mass with a soccer ball under his arm.

The fact that the churchgoers didn't have to cross a doorway to attend the outdoor Mass seemed to contribute to the relaxed atmosphere.

A young woman wore her wedding dress when she came to see Our Lady of the New Millennium and was seen touching her feet and her robe. The young lady was soon to be married, and she wanted to feel that her gown and her marriage were blessed.

Our Lady visits St. Clare of Montefalco parish.

At St. Clare of Montefalco: "What a wonderful two weeks we had! People from all over the neighborhood were drawn to prayer."

Many people who never darken the door of the church came to pray for peace in their homes, for healing, for blessings, and for God's protection for their children. They came expressing deep hopes for a better life, for some help in their present needs, but also expressing their worries and their struggles to believe and hope.

Some walked on their knees over the sidewalks and parking lot to arrive at her feet. They found her to be a consolation that came directly from the Holy Spirit through the powerful intercession of the Blessed Mother.

Countless times during the two weeks, entire families brought flowers, knelt for prayer, and lovingly caressed the image of the Blessed Mother – a simple way to express love and devotion.

Many were drawn to her like a magnet. They stayed and entered the Perpetual Adoration Chapel as well.

People have asked to have their marriages blessed or to marry in the church. Confessions have tripled, and attendance at daily Mass has routinely grown to twenty to twenty-five people, from an earlier four or five.

At Mother of Sorrows Convent, a nun said, "The sisters were happy to see students they had not seen for twenty or thirty years who had come to see the statue. An eleven-year-old boy came with his grandmother. I fell in love with Justin. He presented us with a gift, a musical angel Snow Baby that played 'I Love You from the Bottom of My Heart.' Justin will always be special in my heart."

When Our Lady of the New Millennium spent two weeks at Notre Dame University for the National Medjugorje Conference, thousands came to pray in a steady stream all day and all night. Many said they would like to have the statue installed permanently at Notre Dame.

A young man at Transfiguration Parish blindfolded his girlfriend and brought her to the statue. At the statue's feet, he knelt down, removed the blindfold, and proposed to her. She accepted.

Grace Zizzo was in charge of the statue when it appeared at Festa Italiana on Milwaukee's lakefront. Since she was supposed to "decorate" the statue, she traveled to the previous site to take measurements. However, when she got her first look at the statue, she thought, "I'm supposed to decorate that? It's so beautiful as it is!"

But she noted that Our Lady of the New Millennium did not have a rosary in her hands, so she made one of appropriate size with white roses for the Hail Marys and red roses for the Our Fathers. On the medallion, she placed the cross that had been on her mother's casket.

While the statue was at the Festa, Grace handed out holy cards to the throng. "As I moved around, it seemed like her eyes were moving with me," said Grace. "And, I couldn't believe it, but on her neck I saw the face of Jesus with the crown of thorns. I thought I was hallucinating, but my daughter saw it, too."

Grace commented, "People were so moved when they saw her. She was so large, she was able to hug us all!"

At St. Lambert Parish in Skokie, a deacon said, "The first time I saw it, I was expecting to be overwhelmed by the size. But what struck me was her face. It is not quite happy, not quite sad, but contemplative. It has a lightness to it."

The parish school enrolls students from fifty-one ethnic groups, including Filipinos, Chinese, Luxembourgians, Germans, and small but significant groups of Sri Lankans, Indians, and Haitians, among others. The statue encourages members of the diverse communities that make up the parish to share religious and cultural appreciation of Mary.

One parishioner observed, "Each of our groups has a slightly different tradition, but in sharing this, we became a more united family of faith. As diverse as we are, this is an icon for all the groups."

Another parishioner quoted a Chinese saying as she looked at the statue and the flowers and votive candles surrounding it. "We say that we see her with an ordinary heart. She is one of us, she is our neighbor, and comes to us. She doesn't make us come to her. "We Asians like to see something concrete, to understand the immaterial through the material."

At St. Zachary Church in Des Plaines, countless stories were told by World War II veterans and servicemen and servicewomen from the Korean and Vietnam wars expressing the importance of their faith while they were away from home and the comfort they received by praying the Rosary. Our Lady's statue brought back many memories for them.

A Fresh Start

Visits from Our Lady of the New Millennium became very competitive, and sadly, many parishes and other venues were disappointed when the statue could not satisfy their requests. But one location in Hammond, Indiana received an unexpected and very welcome, visit from The Lady.

After eight years on the road and through all kinds of weather at numerous sites, the statue was in need of a bit of a clean-up. David Van Camp of Van's Industrial, a metal fabricator in Hammond, volunteered to do the job.

Van Camp made the offer for his staff to do the cleaning for a very special reason. He had not been a Catholic all his life. In fact, he had just received the Sacraments of Initiation the previous weekend at St. Maria Goretti in Dyer.

Although he had been married to a "cradle Catholic" for twenty-two years and had raised his three children in the Catholic faith, he had been raised in no religion. But, with no prodding from his wife, Renee, he began questioning life and the afterlife while his father was dying.

He asked Renee numerous questions about the Catholic faith and finally enrolled in the Rite of Christian Initiation of Adults at St. Maria Goretti.

While he was in RCIA training, Renee learned that the giant statue needed cleaning. Although she was not sure how Dave would react, she talked to him about the project.

The couple went to see the statue in Illinois. Renee said, "You know the way God works. Dave was so overwhelmed that day. He felt so blessed. He saw the statue and knew in his heart he wanted to do the cleaning."

Dave talked to his employees about it, made some calls, and everyone volunteered. No one asked for pay.

As a metal fabricator, Van's Industrial was not used to seeing people on its doorstep. But after the statue arrived, as Renee was organizing what was supposed to be a handful of people praying the Rosary, interest grew. Within a short time, there was a small crowd, including numerous children from the area, joining to say the Rosary.

Two small children brought a blanket so they could pray on the concrete. They reminded Francine Demma of the children of Fatima.

Meanwhile, the team at Van's Industrial went to work with long-handled brushes, reverently giving Our Lady of the New Millennium her first thorough cleaning since her completion in 1999.

Renee Van Camp said her husband's interest in Catholicism rekindled her own faith, and she believes the statue is more than just four tons of steel mounted on a semi trailer. Remembering the faces of the people from the neighborhood, she said, "It's brought them hope to say a prayer and look out and see she's looking at us.

"The statue," she said, "was brought to Hammond, to my husband's shop for a bigger reason." She admitted that she didn't know the reason, but one of her husband's employees felt the statue had come full circle. The worker's wife had needed a kidney transplant several years before, and her relatives, using the statue as a source of inspiration, prayed to Mary for a donor. Through an organ transplant, his wife's life was saved.

She said even her husband's demeanor was changed. Previously a skeptical man who saw things only in black and white, David Van Camp allowed the gate to the area where the statue stands to be left open one night. "This is for everyone to share, and in David's own way, he's found time to pray," she said. "We know it's just a statue, but there's more about her. Her presence really makes you think."

Driving Miss Mary

From the time Our Lady of the New Millennium arrived in Chicago, a dedicated and highly skilled professional crew was key to the realization of Carl Demma's dream of taking her to the people of Chicago.

With his many years of experience in the trucking industry, when Marina Cartage owner Mike Tadin saw the statue, he immediately understood the difficulties and challenges that would face a driver transporting her through the streets of the city and into a great variety of challenging locations.

He asked Tom Brischetto to take on this challenge. Brischetto had been driving a truck for 40 years and had worked for Marina Cartage for many of those years. Tom accepted the challenge, and from her first trip to Holy Name Cathedral for Mother's Day, Tom, and later his family, has gotten Our Lady of the New Millennium into some virtually impossible sites, usually at times when most people prefer to be in bed.

He has been called by many "a miracle man" for his expertise in transporting this very special cargo and placing it where even those who saw him do it could hardly believe their eyes as he maneuvered the statue-bearing trailer into almost impossible positions with seeming ease.

The second man Tadin asked to join the team was John Halpin. He had been working for Marina Cartage for eight years, but before that he was Commissioner of Streets and Sanitation for the City of Chicago. Thirty-six of his fifty-nine years in the trucking business had been with the city, beginning as a truck driver. He spent many years dealing with all aspects of the city's road equipment. Halpin became the man in charge of operating the equipment that raises and lowers the statue at each site.

Both men, and those who came later, donated their time to move the statue after their regular workdays.

Halpin explained, "The statue lies on a bed, a cradle. When it reached the location at which it would be erected, I would check that the site was level. There were two dolly legs on each side of the trailer and an outrigger in the center of each side. I employed the hydraulics to extend the outriggers from the chassis to be sure the trailer was on the level. When that was done, I raised the statue and locked it in place, then retracted the cradle. If it wasn't perfectly level, I couldn't lock it in place."

John Halpin handled the mechanics of moving Our Lady from site to site.

Every time the statue was about to move to a new site, Halpin would check out the new location. "I wanted to know where it was going, when it was going, how we would get in, and what to expect at the location. We had to contend with narrow streets and sometimes had to back into the chosen site. Often there were streetlights and telephone wires in the way. At one place we had to hold up the telephone wire with a broom so we could get the trailer into the right spot."

Perhaps the most challenging placement was at Milwaukeefest in Wisconsin. Halpin recalled, "They wanted us to go to a field by the lake, but I didn't think we could make it. You could walk across fine, but the equipment couldn't get traction. We had to put down sheets of plywood under the wheels for more than seventy-five feet. Then we needed a wrecker with a cable to pull us back out."

They were always careful to place the statue so there was an open pathway for people to approach her and to touch her feet.

Halpin didn't travel in the truck with Tom Brischetto, but followed in his own car. The team tried to move the statue early in the morning, usually on Sunday when there was little traffic. "We needed to get to the church before services started and there would be cars in the lot. Several times we moved her at night, arriving at the new church at nine or ten in the evening, and we had to go to work again at two or three in the morning.

"It was a lot of effort, but it seemed like nothing. There was something about that statue that made it worthwhile. I never minded the work, no matter how tired I was."

Halpin noted that the statue is thirteen feet tall when laid horizontal for traveling, and eleven feet, two inches wide. "The toll roads only allowed loads ten feet wide, but they never bothered us," he said.

"When you go out of state, by law, you have to stop to have your truck weighed at a weigh station. I remember pulling into a weigh station at the Wisconsin line. The person on the scale was very generous and told us to move on.

"The police have never bothered us. Gangs are protecting the statue so no one can hurt it. No one has ever harmed it."

He added, "It's been a great pleasure working with Tom Brischetto. He's one of the best!"

Halpin observed, "There is a great devotion to the Blessed Virgin in the Chicago area. Around the clock, wherever we go, people are praying. When we arrive at a new place, there are usually hundreds of people waiting for us, and when we leave, they follow the truck down the street.

"Carl Demma was such a dedicated man and put so much time and effort into building this statue and giving her to the people of Chicago. He wanted everyone to see the statue for free. I think he reached the goal he wanted, and he died happy with it.

"Since his death, his wife, Francine, has gone to every location, talking to everybody about Our Lady of the New Millennium. I've never been to a church that she wasn't there, no matter what time it was. She's a very religious person and is doing a wonderful job in carrying out her husband's dream."

Halpin welcomed the opportunity to provide this service for four years before he retired. "It's a way to express my devotion to the Virgin," he said. "I say my Rosary every day and have a statue in my yard."

Tom Brischetto recalled the first time the statue was erected, upon its arrival at Marina Cartage. "The Archdiocese had a lawyer, an insurance person, and another person here. When they saw the statue, they were flabbergasted. They called Bishop Goedert who wanted them to take it down to Holy Name Cathedral - immediately.

The next day, Brischetto drove Our Lady of the New Millennium to her first visitation.

For the first time, Halpin attached the hoses for the hydraulic system to the tractor to raise the statue. He leveled the truck and extended the outriggers to brace it as Carl and Fran Demma, some of their friends, and members of the clergy looked on.

After Halpin's retirement, the job of raising the statue was taken on by Robert Jett for a short time, and then Brischetto's son-in-law, Ken Krzak. Transporting the statue became a family affair. Tom's wife, Carol, their daughter, Amy, and their granddaughter, Emily, often rode in the escort car.

"We go to the church where the statue has been appearing and take it down," said Brischetto. "When it's time to leave the church, we put the emergency lights on our cars that will be following the trailer. We have CB radios in case we should run into a roadblock or other safety situation. Our route is all figured out in advance, so it's not usually a problem."

Often he does a dry run in advance to check whether the lot is level, if it's wide enough, whether there are overhanging trees, low wires, or viaducts to contend with.

Driver Tom Brischetto

He said, "I try to find just where they might want to put it so we can take it right to the spot where they want it. But when we arrive, they may tell me to move it three feet in one direction or try a different corner. Sometimes I have to move it ten times before I have it where they want it. Once it is set up, it doesn't move until it comes down.

"If at all possible, we try to place it so it's facing the church, unless they want something different."

Brischetto has faced some very big challenges in placing Our Lady of the New Millennium, but none greater than at the church that is attended by Chicago Mayor Richard M. Daley. "The parking lot was very narrow," he recalled, "and we had to go up on the sidewalk and jackknife the rig to get it in place. I kept thinking, 'We don't want to mess this one up!' Then I wondered how we were going to get it out. We managed okay, but it was a tight maneuver."

Setting up the statue includes placing a rosary in the hands of the statue – sometimes the one that travels in the truck, and sometimes one provided by the people of the parish. Before she is raised, a crown of flowers is often placed on her head.

Raising the statue and putting it up takes about twenty minutes.

At one location, as the statue was raised, water fell from her eyes. Some exclaimed, "She's crying!" but were quickly reminded that it had rained a little while before, and water had collected in the cavities of her eyes.

Brischetto said, "I see the people, their faces, and how happy they are to see the statue. They find a lot of peace in the statue. She does that for me, so I know how it must be for these people.

"They come on crutches, in wheelchairs. She has brought a lot of people together.

"By the time we take the statue down, there are notes stuffed into the robes of the statue. They say, 'Help my mother,' 'Help my dad,' 'Help my sister.' The notes fall out, and we pick them up and give them to the priest.

"If you have any kind of heart, when you see this, you know why we have to keep this going. Somehow it's going to help them, and we want to do it."

They have transported Our Lady of the New Millennium to a number of high crime areas, but for the week she's been there, there's been no crime. The neighborhood gang members have been guarding the statue, keeping things quiet in the neighborhood while the statue was there.

"People want to find out all about the statue," said Brischetto, "They can't thank Francine enough – they feel she's a great lady.

"When Carl was alive, he loved seeing people enjoy his creation. When he saw how happy people were, all praying, he lit up like a Christmas tree. He was an amazing guy.

"It's an honor for me to do this. Carl appreciated my doing it, and I know Fran appreciates it.

"It's not an easy thing to learn how to put the statue up and down, so it's important to know what you're doing. It's not like you could just take it to a body shop for repairs if it were damaged. This is a unique and precious thing.

"I guess I'm a dedicated person. I'm kind of proud to do it. When I see the kids' faces, I think, 'This kid is going to remember this statue for the rest of his life.'

"That makes me feel good."

A Knight's Crusade

Philip A. Krueger was long concerned that Rosary devotion was no longer being spread to young Catholics, and he wanted to do something about it. Krueger was Grand Knight of Holy Rosary Council 4493 of the Knights of Columbus in Arlington Heights, Illinois.

He and the Knights were already spreading devotion by holding monthly public Rosary recitation. Between eighty-five and one hundred parishioners generally attended, but few younger Catholics came.

In May, 2000 – Mary's month – Krueger asked Cardinal George if the Knights could visit archdiocesan schools and distribute rosaries to students. The cardinal told Krueger that another man, Carl Demma, had recently approached the diocese with a similar request. He told Krueger about Demma's commission of the construction of an 8,400-pound stainless steel statue of Mary and of the scheduled visits to parishes throughout metropolitan Chicago to inspire devotion to Mary, especially among youth.

Krueger was impressed with Demma's project. When he learned Demma also wanted to provide free rosaries so children could pray the Rosary with their parents, he felt the Knights and Demma had to join forces.

He contacted Fr. John P. Smyth, former University of Notre Dame basketball All-American and current director of Maryville Academy, a home for troubled youth in Des Plaines, Illinois. Maryville's spacious main campus was thought to be the perfect location for the Knight's May crowning of Demma's huge statue.

On May 13, more than fifteen hundred of the faithful took part in the May crowning. The procession began with a bagpipe band followed by more than one hundred children from across the archdiocese who had won a Marian-themed coloring contest devised by Krueger.

Next came fifty-four Knights from fifteen councils and eight assemblies.

A forecast of high winds and showers prompted Krueger to crown the thirty-three-foot statue earlier in the week. The crown of flowers was woven by members of Holy Rosary Council's women's group. A twenty-foot rosary was placed in the statue's hands. At that moment, the sun shone briefly, reflecting the K of C medallion on the rosary.

After the recitation of the Memorare, the clergy took turns leading the Rosary. A concelebrated Mass concluded the afternoon's activities.

By the end of the weekend, all of the 8,500 rosaries Krueger had brought were claimed. Not only had each child in attendance taken one, but many had taken extras for their siblings and friends.

Kenosha Celebrates 100 Years

In 1903, Italian immigrants settled in the Upper Peninsula of Michigan. The next year, because copper mines were closing and work was hard to find, many came to Kenosha, Wisconsin, to work in the factories.

They became members of the small mission church of Our Lady of Pompeii. Classes were held so they could learn English, and athletic teams were formed. Those with a love of music started a Holy Rosary band.

A new church was completed in 1931, and a school was built in 1953, staffed by nuns and lay teachers. In 1999, the church and school were renovated.

Our Lady of the New Millennium went to Kenosha in July, 2004 to help celebrate the one-hundred-year history of Our Lady of Pompeii of the Holy Rosary Church. Few people in Kenosha will ever forget that week.

Kathy Del Conte, who works with the youth of the church, hoped the arrival of the statue would attract teenagers to the church. "But there wasn't a teen in sight," she said. "Then, gradually, they started trickling out to join the hundreds already there."

The day before the statue arrived, there had been a wedding at the church, and the bridal family donated all of the flowers.

Many people helped by putting up chairs in front of the statue; even kindergartners helped.

One night a large number of children arrived and asked if there was anything for them. They were told, "I can't give you a rosary until I tell you a story." Then they heard the story about Mary's treasure box, told by a graduate of the school, speaking as Mary. As she took items out of the box, she explained how each was related to Jesus. This story was repeated numerous times during the week.

The children received some of the 10,500 rosaries that had been donated by the Blue Army and from Holy Cross Family Ministries. Although carefully rationed, there were not enough to last the entire week.

People continued to bring flowers and then fall on their knees and pray. One basket of flowers was sent by the parishioners of another church.

A special guest at Our Lady of Pompeii of the Holy Rosary's Centennial Celebration. Photo by Sam Lucero.

There was a living Rosary. People walked in a circle, and every time they said a "Hail Mary," they moved a space.

One night, no Rosary was scheduled. People approached and asked, "Aren't we going to have a Rosary?" So two young girls got up and led it.

A man standing next to a sister told her that he knew he was supposed to say the Rosary, but never did. He had been taught how to do it, but never took the time. He told the sister, "I am a changed person. Now I will say it every day."

One night, Eleanor Staves, who works at the church, couldn't sleep. About three a.m. she got up and went to the statue. "I was surprised how many people were there at that hour," she said.

"Even then, there was a holy atmosphere, aided by the music that was playing the entire time."

The statue had been lit entirely with blue lights, giving an aspect so unique that it was featured in the Catholic Herald in Milwaukee.

Afterwards, a woman wrote, "That was the most inspiring thing I have seen since the birth of my child twelve years ago."

One member of the parish commented, "As many non-Catholics as Catholics came to see her. She caused the whole city to be one community."

David Simonetti Has a Dream

David Simonetti was teaching at Noonan Elementary Academy, a private Catholic school in Mokena, Illinois, when students came into class one morning talking about the new statue they had seen the night before. They related how giant she was, even her toes!

Simonetti recalled seeing Carl Demma on the news when Pope John Paul II blessed the statue in St. Louis, and he had seen other articles and pictures of this statue. He was anxious to see this monumental work for himself.

He recalls driving into the parking lot at St. Germaine Church. "What I saw before me was hard to believe," he recalls. "Before us was a shining tower of graced love, an almost unbelievable image of our Mother Most Beautiful."

A few months later, he saw her again at St. Rocco Oratory in Chicago Heights. He said, "Pulling up in the drive at the oratory, you beheld Mary, the Mother of God, shining in the sun at the end of a long, narrow walkway against the backdrop of a rich blue sky. She towered like the pillar of fire, a cloud of smoke from the days of Exodus in the Old Testament. Alongside her at the base in a perfectly balanced divide were the Stations of the Cross. That caught one breathless."

He thought to himself, "Can you imagine how beautiful the real Blessed Mother must be like in heaven if this image is so heart moving?"

He heard a man remark, "A sculptor didn't make that statue. God made that!"

The following year, Simonetti began his studies for the priesthood at the University of St. Mary of the Lake (Mundelein Seminary), and he again saw Our Lady of the New Millennium at the celebration of the Walk of Faith.

"In the daytime, I would sit in front of her, and then again when it was very peaceful and quiet at night. As a seminarian, I felt a great desire to offer a Mass one day before her. It became a great dream in my life."

He nurtured his dream all during his studies in the next six years. After ordination, he began serving at Queen of Martyrs Parish. When he learned that Our Lady of the New Millennium was to visit his parish, it brought him a joy he couldn't describe.

People came in a steady stream of faith as she beamed and shone as a great tower of beauty and love. As Simonetti talked with Francine Demma, a barrage of fireworks exploded, showering blazing patterns in the sky.

The next day, Simonetti's dream, cherished for six years, came true. He was granted the gift of concelebrating the Eucharist with a special friend, Fr. James Hollup. During the Mass, Simonetti kept turning to Our Lady and trying to convince

David Simonetti realizes his dream of celebrating Mass before Our Lady.

himself, “This is really happening! She is here, and I am celebrating the Mass in front of her with a priest who is most special to me!”

The next two weeks were filled with unforgettable memories and joy, including three more occasions on which Simonetti said Mass before Our Lady of the New Millennium. One was a healing Mass with over eight hundred in attendance.

Simonetti found great joy in sitting outside by the street in the evening watching people drive by and look at the image. He observed people coming just to sit in silence and pray before her with hope in their hearts.

Many would drive by and honk to say hello to her, and he could hear others excitedly talking about what they were seeing, almost in disbelief. He saw people of many faiths drawn to her because her universal motherhood was transmitted to their hearts, transcending all faiths and peoples.

After the closing liturgy before the statue was to depart, Simonetti knelt down and thanked her for everything she had given in the past two weeks.

He said, “The statue of Our Lady of the New Millennium is meant to bring people together, to bring a community of faith together in prayer to God. That is what has happened. So many graces have been showered down upon us, so many prayers heard and answered, and so many more still to be received.

“The statue is gone now, and there is a small hollow ache in the heart when one looks into the empty parking lot where she stood. What can one say for consolation but perhaps just repeat the words of our Blessed Lord Himself, ‘Behold your Mother!’”

New Life After the Tornado

There are many special things about St. Mary Immaculate Parish in Plainfield, Illinois.

With twenty-five thousand members, it is the largest parish in the Joliet diocese.

Eighty percent of the parishioners are forty years or younger, and forty percent of the parish family is under eighteen years old.

The pastor, Father David Medow, a former Lutheran minister, is also the first married priest in the Joliet Diocese.

Plainfield, in which the parish is located, is the fastest growing town in the Midwest.

But most memorable for the members of St. Mary Immaculate Parish and the Plainfield area is the day – August 28, 1990 – when one of the most powerful tornadoes ever to strike northern Illinois ripped through Plainfield. It destroyed the church, the school and the rectory, killing the principal of the parish school, the music teacher, and another parishioner.

The response of the members of the parish was to build a new school, church, and rectory at a cost of $6.5 million.

Membership of the parish has exploded from two thousand families to over six thousand eight hundred.

So, when the church members received word from Francine Demma that Our Lady of the New Millennium would come to St. Mary Immaculate for two weeks during October, there was great joy and also an immediate determination to make the most of this special opportunity.

A team was formed to oversee the events of her visit. One

team developed a schedule of rituals for each day, and another developed prayer resources and candles that could be used on site or at home.

The members of the publicity team contacted every publicity outlet they could find.

St. Mary Immaculate has over one hundred ministries in the church, from the Knights of Columbus and St. Mary's Seniors to adult enrichment programs and a M.O.M.s group. Each ministry was asked to lead one of the rituals during the two weeks. There were five or six events each day, beginning in the morning, and at night, Rosaries and benedictions, with Mass some nights.

Two evenings, auxiliary bishops led processions and benedictions. Every class in the parish school and every grade level in the religious education program played a role, as did each family in the parish that was homeschooling its children.

Reconciliation was offered every day, and other priests came in to help.

Thousands of people came each day. A seating area was provided twenty-four hours a day, seven days a week, with willing parishioners on hand to welcome visitors.

St. Mary Immaculate is located on Illinois Rt. 59, a very busy road. When people driving by saw the statue, many pulled into the parking lot.

Father David said, "The parish had gone through some times of conflict, but now we're writing a new chapter. The statue has helped to bring us together.

"The whole month of October was used as a month of prayer, and there was a visioning process for the entire parish. It seemed Mrs. Demma's permission came out of nowhere, and we felt it was Our Lady's way of endorsing our month of prayer and planning. It proved an incredibly fruitful time.

"Our vision was of one family in faith making Christ known and embraced by His parish as a whole. This has become the template by which we plan all of our ministries and evaluate our success."

The new vision is exemplified in a new logo one team developed. A very talented group of people put together a stunning twenty-page booklet with dozens of pictures of the statue's visit and numerous prayers, including the Memorare, A Prayer to Our Lady of Guadalupe, and a prayer written by a bishop of the diocese.

People from other churches came, some who were lapsed Catholics. Besides bringing together people from other parishes and other faiths, the visit of Our Lady of the New Millennium was an inter-generational experience, uniting people of all ages.

Some families gathered by the statue to pray the Rosary and have continued that practice at home.

Father David said, "No one was worshiping the statue. Her presence prompts conversation. The statue makes the presence of Our Lady in our lives very real. People see her as a friend and as a mother. Prayer is a conversation with God, and she prompts that conversation. That's why the statue has touched so many people's hearts and lives. It is an effective presence."

"She was a gathering point," said Father David, "inviting people to her Son. She invited the practice of prayer as a deeper part of the life of our school and our parish."

Francine

Born in Chicago, just two blocks from Chinatown, where her father, Rosario DiGiacomo, owned a movie theater, Francine DiGiacomo attended Catholic grammar school where Mass was said every day.

Francine with her daughters, Carla and Judi, 1965.

"We were taught by Notre Dame nuns," she recalls, "and they were great teaching nuns! Every year, Mary's month of May was devoted to the Blessed Mother, and May crownings were held."

The family attended Santa Maria Incoronata Church. Her mother, Florence, was a very devoted Catholic.

When Francine was sixteen, her first date with Carl Demma was at Soldier Field where they went for the stock car races. She would reflect later that the last time they went out together it was also to Soldier Field for the Field of Faith celebration.

She worked at Northern Illinois Bank as a supervisor of the IBM proof department and the bookkeeping department for a number of years. She also worked at Harris Trust. Francine served as property manager in her family's real estate business. For ten years, she worked part time as an intake worker for the Crisis Center of South Suburbia.

Francine's devotion to her husband and her family were tested severely many times, especially during the illness and deaths of her daughters.

She was tested again when Carl felt it was time to honor the commitment he had made when he was ten years old – to build a huge statue of the Blessed Mother for the people of Chicago.

"I felt overwhelmed," said Francine. "I couldn't imagine him doing something like this.

"He talked about it and talked about it and talked about it. He started talking to everyone he met. I wondered if they thought he was crazy, but I just stayed in the background, taking it all in. And I found they were listening.

"He was a good storyteller, but I couldn't help thinking this could never happen. There were too many things against him. He wasn't a well man, and I worried so about the things he would have to go through."

After Charles Parks began work on Our Lady of the New Millennium, money would run out. When people inquired about the statue, Francine would say it was "in limbo."

But in 1998, when she traveled with Carl to Padua, and then after the subsequent sale of his business, she knew it was real, that it was truly going to happen.

However, the enormity of the statue continued to be overwhelming to her. Francine asked Carl, "Wouldn't it be easier to transport if it were not so big?" He said that it would have to be very large in order to have a very large impact.

After it was completed, she worried constantly that there could be a problem when it was being raised and lowered. Then she questioned whether it was necessary to take it to so many locations.

But Carl's faith led her, and in faith and love, she followed and supported his dream. "I had such pride in him, I couldn't have stopped him," she said.

"I think he always knew what it could do, and what it would do. He was a man who had the gift of our faith. You meet a lot of people who are religious, but not as gifted as he was.

"We would speak about God, and he always spoke from his

heart. People could sense that about him. He didn't question; he wasn't fanatical. He believed in living the Gospels."

When Carl died, it was uncertain whether Our Lady of the New Millennium would continue her travels. The original goal was for the statue to move for two years, and then find a permanent home. She had been traveling for a year when Carl passed away.

Although a very dynamic woman, Francine was not a person to "take over," but she was called to do just that when Carl was gone. Francine conferred with the Cardinal and agreed to honor the remaining schedule for the year 2000 as well as the commitments that had been set for 2001. As the enthusiasm and excitement about the statue's visits continued to grow rather than wane, Francine Demma continued to arrange for it to be taken to the people, as Carl had wanted. By then, Francine was deeply involved in the scheduling. She went to every location where the statue went, talking to people eager to learn more about her and about Our Lady of the New Millennium.

Tom Brischetto said, "Fran would come to our house, or we'd pick her up about three in the morning. She makes the arrangements with the church or whatever our destination is to be. She calls me, and I call back to the contact there.

"While the men are erecting the statue, Francine is greeting the many people who want to meet her and learn more about the statue."

After the statue had visited one parish, a man wrote, "You are someone whom we will never forget. Your candidness is something we will always remember. Your passion and kindness are an inspiration to all!"

Photographer Oscar Mendez observed, "When Mr. Demma died, I'm sure he was confident that his wife was going to continue. I imagine it's been very hard for her. She's doing great things. We don't realize what energy she needs to do the work she's doing, but with the grace of God, we can do anything when God is beside us.

"She has a great faith in the Virgin Mary and a very strong, powerful love of Jesus. Mrs. Demma has been an inspiration to many of us. She's so humble, so selfless. She cares about people. They like her because she loves to talk about God and about the Virgin Mary."

With a smile, Francine recalls the little boy who queried, "If Mary is as big as this, how big can Jesus be?"

Or the young boy who, seeing the statue, exclaimed, "Whoa!!", then turned to her and said, "And I mean that in a good way!"

She will never forget the evening she had visited a priest at Sacred Heart Parish in Palos Hills who was recovering from surgery. When leaving, she gave printed holy cards to two Hispanic women with a child and asked if it was the first time they had seen the statue. One of the women noted that she had seen it at another parish, but that she was very concerned about her son who had been talking about suicide, and she had come to be with the statue for the comfort it gave her.

When on an airplane en route to Lourdes, Francine was talking with a lady sitting next to her who said she was from Elmwood Park, Illinois. Fran asked if she had seen the statue when it had been at a church there three months before. The lady, Fonti Fontanilla, pulled out her cell phone and showed Fran the picture on it – Our Lady of the New Millennium.

Fran said, "Today we're very good friends. I've made so very many friends among the people who have come to see the statue."

Irena Gavaghan recalls meeting Francine at Sacred Heart Parish two days after the day set aside for Polish people. She had invited her daughters and their friends to wear traditional Polish costumes and to attend this special day for the Polish people to recognize the Black Madonna of Czestochowa.

Irena shared her experiences with the Holy Spirit and Padre Pio, and Francine gave her daughter, Victoria, a beautiful rosary.

Irena says, "We have since made many trips together, including a trip to Rome in 2002 for the canonization of Padre Pio." Two years later they returned to the Vatican for Easter. They met Bishop Stanislaw Dziwisz, who remembered the blessing of the statue in St. Louis by Pope John Paul II.

After this encounter, they had an audience with the Holy Father, giving him a picture of Our Lady of the New Millennium.

Irena says, "Being with Fran has brought much joy and happiness to me, my husband, Brian, and our daughters. Fran is a person who gives this joy and happiness freely to other people. I am honored to be her friend."

Everywhere she goes, people tell Francine, "I met your husband," or "Your husband gave me holy cards." They touch her arm and tell her they are praying for her. She said, "They are always sharing stories about him. People are always talking about him and sharing beautiful feelings."

Fr. Tony Markus, a close friend, said, "Francine is very generous, very kind, easy to talk to, and always smiling. If a wrench is thrown in, she accepts that it is meant to be. She doesn't have great frustration because her strong faith helps her."

Francine Demma's many contributions to her church and her community include serving on the Board of Directors of the Crisis Center of South Suburbia. She is a member of the Blue Army of Fatima, the Order of Sons of Italy, and the Presentation Choir.

She serves at a soup kitchen, participates in the Cuddles Program for babies, and leads prayer groups at nursing homes. Fran said, "I think throughout my life I have been led, getting me prepared for the responsibilities of Our Lady of the New Millennium."

When Francine was in Washington, D.C. for a pro-life event, she met with her congressman, Daniel Lipinski, and told him about Carl and about the statue. Shortly thereafter, Congressman Lipinski stood on the floor of the U.S. House of Representatives and told Carl's story.

The congressman said, "Mr. Speaker, I applaud Mr. and Mrs. Demma for their dedication and their many years of service to the community."

The Speaker, Congressman Dennis Hastert, replied, "May Our Lady of the New Millennium bless the District of Illinois."

Francine is honored by the Italian Cultural Center as 2002 Woman of the year. Shown here with Fr. Gino Del Paiz.

St. Joseph Seminary awarded Francine Demma its Mater Dei Award, given annually to a woman or group who respond generously to the call to service in the Lord and His Church. The Mater Dei Award was established twelve years ago because of the need to highlight women role models who have made significant contributions to the service of God's people. The celebration honoring Francine drew the largest attendance in its history.

She also received the 2002 Woman of the Year Award from the Italian Cultural Center, where it was noted, "Francine's determination to carry out the legacy that her husband, Carl, started demonstrates her strength of faith and devotion to the Blessed Mother. She is a very special person who inspires us, not only through her shining example, but through her family's offering of the Our Lady of the New Millennium statue to the community."

In 2005, the Shrine of Our Lady of Pompeii honored Francine, and also Carl, with the Holy Mother Humanitarian Award, which is given to individuals whose entire lives embody the qualities of Mary, the Mother of God, because of their dedication to Our Lady of the New Millennium.

Francine declared, "Ensuring that Carl's dream does not die has kept him alive for me. It has given me great healing. I feel his presence everywhere."

Memorable Moments

Gloria Bagadiong related, "When Our Lady was at our parish, I was responsible for collecting the money from donations and the sales of candles while she was here, and I was with her every day from seven in the morning until midnight.

"One Saturday evening, I collected the money and put the receipts from candles, about $500, in one envelope and the donations, about $600, in another. Since the rectory was closed, I put the two envelopes in my pocket when I left to have dinner with a friend.

"When we reached the restaurant, I felt in my pocket – the envelopes were gone. I checked the car, but couldn't find them.

"I couldn't enjoy my dinner. I kept asking myself how I would be able to replace the money. I prayed to Our Lady of the New Millennium to help me. I didn't tell my friend, but she sensed my mood and asked why I was so sad. I told her I just wasn't in the mood for a festive dinner, and I kept praying.

"Early the next morning, I turned on the light at the church parking lot near Our Lady. I began to check that everything was in order. I knelt at the feet of Our Lady and prayed, 'Please show me where the money is. People will think I stole the money.'

"Although the wind had not been blowing, I suddenly saw some gusts of wind. It blew so hard, I felt it was pulling me. I asked Our Lady, 'Is this something you are showing me?'

"All of the leaves had blown in one direction, and I went with the wind and the leaves. When I reached the corner of the parking lot, I saw two envelopes standing there. They weren't even sealed.

"The wind and Our Lady had guided me to them. All the money was there."

When Alice Fallon of St. Rosalie Parish had a difficult and frustrating family situation, she returned to the statue many times to pray, placing her petitions in the Blessed Mother's hands. When her prayers were answered, Alice contemplated how to show her appreciation for the answer to her prayers.

She decided to purchase one thousand medals and share them with people she met. Going one step further, she took the medals to the statue's location at St. Thomas More Parish and had the medals blessed at the feet of Our Lady.

People of all faiths welcomed the medals, and Alice heard stories from people who had received them.

A friend's granddaughter was born with many complications and was in the ICU for a very long time. Alice was told that, through the medal and many prayers, the baby's health improved, and at five years, she was doing very well.

An acquaintance with a brain tumor has survived against all odds. She had received a medal and many prayers.

A young man had applied for a job with the Chicago Police Department and was waiting for a call that he was accepted. Not only did he get the job, he even got his retired father's star number. He carries his medal always.

A good friend who is of another faith went with Alice to see Our Lady. The friend is recovering from breast cancer. She carries her medal and a breast cancer pin with her through every treatment and surgery. She was ecstatic to have the opportunity to pray and thank Our Lady.

Alice wrote to Francine Demma, "I will forever bless the day that Our Lady of the New Millennium came into my life and the lives of others. My prayers are with you and your wonderful husband in heaven, who has made this possible for all of us."

At San Rocco Oratory, Lou Pignotti was handing out literature when he saw a woman get out of her car, talking loudly to the people in the car. She was smoking, and he felt she was dressed inappropriately. He recalls thinking to himself, "You don't belong here. This is not a carnival, and there's no liquor here."

He spent fifteen minutes greeting other visitors and then glanced over and caught sight of a figure way to the side. Kneeling all alone in the grass was the woman he had believed had no business there. She was on her knees with tears streaming down, her eyes fixed on Our Lady of the New Millennium.

Lou said, "It was as if God was telling me, 'Only I know the true heart of my daughter and the true heart of all of my children. You are not to judge anyone.'

"I was truly humbled. I realized that seeing this woman and feeling the way I did was a gift from God through the powerful intercession of our Blessed Mother.

"This woman I judged so harshly was a sight to see and a sight I needed to see. For me it was a spiritual healing. It was a beautiful day."

Ana M.'s son, Benjamin, had been looking for employment for about a year. Ana went to pray to Our Lady of the New Millennium that he would be able to get a job and asked that her son have the ability to answer all the questions correctly to get the job for which he was interviewing.

The same day, Benjamin successfully went through an interview with a prospective employer, and then a second interview.

When he came home that evening, he reported that he had been hired on the spot.

Then Benjamin, who is one of little faith, disappeared for a few minutes and returned with a huge bouquet of roses in his arms. He said that they were for Our Lady of the New Millennium. He felt the bouquet of roses was the least he could do for the grand miracle she had done for him.

He told Ana that he, too, had gone and prayed that he get the job. "This was the greatest miracle of all," she said.

Dotti Nichols was in great turmoil when her gravely ill husband was hospitalized with breathing problems. She was told he would not be admitted to a nursing home, as he was not expected to live. Home aid was prohibitively expensive. Dotti sat in his hospital room in tears.

A floor nurse came to her and said that hospice people would give a few hours a day, but she would need other help. Dotti spent the night at her sister's home, and they discussed her dilemma.

The following morning, she drove back to the hospital. On the way, she passed Our Lady of the New Millennium, which was at that time at Marytown Academy in Libertyville. Dotti cried and prayed, "Mother Mary, you are the only one who can help me now. I don't know what to do. Please help me to help my husband."

At the hospital, the same floor nurse asked if she was willing to put her husband in a hospice unit at another hospital. When Dotti replied in the affirmative, the nurse called a hospital social worker, who made the arrangements. Dotti's husband was quickly transferred and passed away peacefully four days later with Dotti at his side.

The following week, she returned to the first hospital to thank the nurse who had helped her so much. She could find no one who knew of this nurse on the cardiac ward.

Dotti said, "I believe she was an angel sent by Our Lady of the New Millennium to help me in my hour of great need."

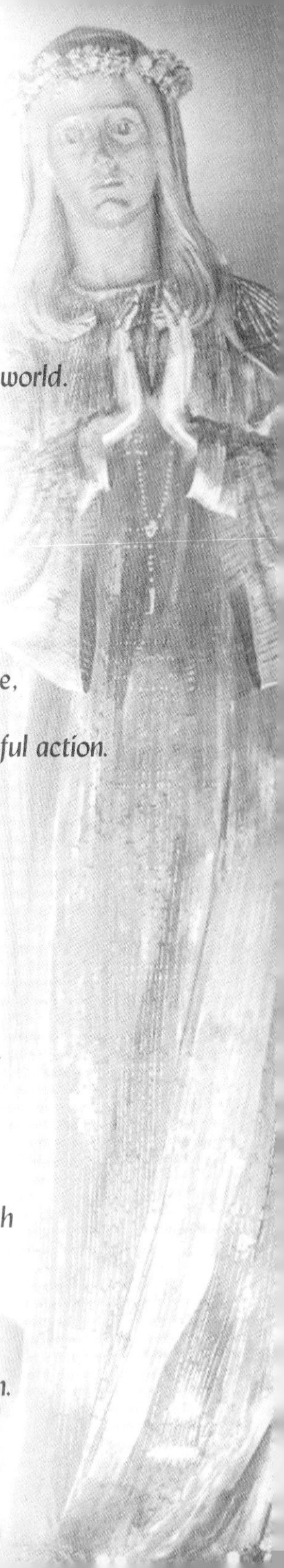

Prayer to Our Lady of the New Millennium

By Pope John Paul II

Mother of the Redeemer,
With great joy we call you blessed.

In order to carry out His plan of salvation,
God the Father chose you before the creation of the world.
You believed in His love and obeyed His word.

The Son of God desired you for His Mother
When He became man
To save the human race.
You received Him with ready obedience
And undivided heart.

The Holy Spirit loved you as His mystical spouse,
And He filled you with singular gifts.
You allowed yourself to be led by His hidden and powerful action.

On the eve of the third Christian Millennium,
We entrust to you the Church
Which acknowledges you
And invokes you as Mother.

To you, Mother of the human family
And of the nations,
We confidently entrust the whole of humanity,
With its hopes and fears.
Do not let it lack the light of true wisdom.

Guide its steps in the ways of peace.
Enable all to meet Christ, the Way and the Truth
And the Life.

Sustain us, O Virgin Mary
On our journey of faith
And obtain for us the grace of eternal salvation.
O clement, O loving, O sweet Mother of God
And our Mother, Mary!

Epilogue

The story of Our Lady of the New Millennium is far from over. While this book is being published, the statue continues to travel to parishes, to share her blessings with all those she touches. Meanwhile, work continues to find a permanent home for Our Lady, where she will carry on Carl Demma's dream of inspiring devotion to the Blessed Mother.

For the current location of Our Lady of the New Millennium, please refer to the Archdiocese of Chicago's website at www.archdiocese-chgo.org/olotm.shtm or the statue's site at www.ourladyofthemillennium.com.

About the Author

Gail Jardine was a newspaper reporter, author, and owner of Newsletters, Ltd., a corporate newsletter service. As a very spiritual person, Gail was very excited to begin work on this book as soon as the opportunity was presented. She painstakingly interviewed each contributor, traveling throughout the Chicago area to do so. She also went to Delaware specifically to meet with the sculptor, Charles Parks.

Through her research, Gail was able to garner a strong feeling about Our Lady of the New Millennium's story; what she means to those who visit her, and the graces she bestows. Gail gave selflessly in the pursuit of telling this story. She put her heart and soul into this work, and very much looked forward to seeing the final product. Sadly, after over two years of work, Gail's health began to fail, and she passed away on January 17, 2009, just after completing the book.

When Gail wasn't busy writing one of her books or corporate newsletters she enjoyed spending time at her family cottage in Door County, Wisconsin. She could frequently be found reading a good book in her favorite chair or enjoying the beautiful scenery.

Those who knew Gail would tell you that she lived her life with great passion!

In Loving Memory of
Gail Jardine
January 21, 1932 - January 17, 2009